LITERACY PLAY FOR THE EARLY YEARS
Book 4

Learning through phonics

BOWLING GREEN STATE UNIVERSITY
DISCARDED
LIBRARY

COLLETTE DRIFTE

David Fulton Publishers
London

BOWLING GREEN STATE
UNIVERSITY LIBRARIES

For my Mum

David Fulton Publishers Ltd
The Chiswick Centre, 414 Chiswick High Road, London W4 5TF

www.fultonpublishers.co.uk

David Fulton Publishers is a division of Granada Learning Limited, part of the Granada Media group.

First published in Great Britain by David Fulton Publishers 2003
10 9 8 7 6 5 4 3 2 1

Note: the right of Collette Drifte to be identified as the author of this work has been asserted by her in accordance with the Copyright, Designs and Patents Act 1988.

Copyright © Collette Drifte 2003
Illustrations © Ella Burfoot 2003, Graham-Cameron Illustration

British Library Cataloguing in Publication Data
A catalogue record for this book is available from the British Library.

ISBN 1-85346-959-9

The materials in this publication may be photocopied only for use within the purchasing organisation. Otherwise, all rights reserved. No part of this publication may be reproduced, stored in a retrieval system or transmitted, in any form or by any means, electronic, mechanical, photocopying, or otherwise, without the prior permission of the publishers.

Also available in the **Literacy Play for the Early Years** series:

Book 1: *Learning through fiction* ISBN 1-85346-956-4
Book 2: *Learning through non-fiction* ISBN 1-85346-957-2
Book 3: *Learning through poetry* ISBN 1-85346-958-0

Cover design by Phil Barker
Designed and typeset by FiSH Books, London
Printed and bound in Great Britain by Thanet Press Limited, Margate, Kent
Audio recording for the CD by Serendipity
CD voice-over by Jane Bower

CURR
372.21
D779Lph

Contents

Acknowledgements iv

Introduction 1

1 Foundation stage and Reception Year 6

Auditory awareness and auditory discrimination of environmental sounds 7

Auditory awareness and auditory discrimination of instrumental sounds 10

Auditory awareness and auditory discrimination of body sounds 13

Auditory awareness and auditory discrimination of speech and voice sounds 16

Rhythm, rhyme and alliteration 19

Single phonemes *a–z*, *ch*, *sh* and *th* 24

CVC words, onset and rime 29

2 Year 1 45

Medial vowels 46

Final consonant digraphs 49

Initial consonant blends and clusters 54

Final consonant blends and clusters 61

Long vowels 65

3 Year 2 75

Vowel phonemes *oo* (short as in *good*), *ar*, *oy/oi* and *ow/ou* 76

Vowel phonemes *air/are/ere/ear* (as in *bear*), *or/oor/au/aw/ore* and *er/ir/ur* 82

Consonant digraphs *wh*, *ph* and *ch* (as in *Christopher*) 85

Vowel phonemes *ear* (as in *hear*) and *ea* (as in *head*) 88

Compound words 91

Observation and assessment for speaking and listening 97

Observation and assessment for reading and writing 98

Tracks and/or transcript for the accompanying CD 99

Acknowledgements

I should like to thank the following for their support and encouragement throughout the writing of this book: Helen Fairlie of David Fulton Publishers for her sound suggestions and professional friendliness; Alan Worth, also of David Fulton Publishers, for seeing the book through the production process; Sophie Cox for her excellent copy-editing; friends and professionals who tried out the activities and made suggestions; the children's parents; and, finally, but probably most important of all, the children themselves. Some of them feature in the little scenarios but, for reasons of confidentiality, their names and details have been altered.

Collette Drifte

Introduction

Curriculum guidance for the foundation stage, the *National Literacy Strategy* and learning through play

Many early years practitioners find it difficult to reconcile the Early learning goals of the foundation stage and the objectives of the *National Literacy Strategy* (DfEE 1998). The philosophy of learning through play is emphasised in *Curriculum guidance for the foundation stage* (DfEE 2000) and rightly so – it is beyond question that young children learn both more, and more effectively, through involvement in activities that are enjoyable, fun, and contain an element of play. The *National Literacy Strategy* (*NLS*) document outlines its objectives without touching on this in any depth and the practitioner may perhaps feel that it is a sterile document in terms of addressing the concept of learning through play. But the two documents aren't mutually exclusive and they can live alongside each other fairly well, since many of the *NLS* objectives do actually tie in with the Early learning goals.

For example,

Early learning goals from *Curriculum guidance for the foundation stage,* Communication, language and literacy:

- Listen with enjoyment, and respond to . . . songs . . . rhymes and poems and make up their own . . . songs, rhymes and poems.
- Explore and experiment with sounds, words and texts.

Objectives from the *National Literacy Strategy (YR)*:

- To understand and be able to rhyme through recognising, exploring and working with rhyming patterns.
- To reread and recite stories and rhymes with predictable and repeated patterns and experiment with similar rhyming patterns.

Lisa, the Learning Support Assistant (LSA), shares a book of rhymes and poems with Leo, Gita, Ben and Paddy. They look at the illustration of *Twinkle, twinkle, little star* and then recite the familiar rhyme together. Lisa says, 'Let's change the rhyme a bit and make a funny one of our own. Can you think of a rhyming word to finish this one? – OK, now listen: *Twinkle, twinkle, little star, I can put you in a . . .*'

Leo shouts, 'Car' and Paddy says, 'Jar'. The children and Lisa all recite the two verses of their new rhyme together. In this scenario, the Foundation stage goals and *NLS* objectives listed above have been achieved.

Advisers and inspectors are recommending that early years practitioners give priority to the *Curriculum guidance for the foundation stage* in their setting, so the children should not lose out on either the stepping stones or the learning through play philosophy. As long as you plan your activities within the framework of *Curriculum guidance for the foundation stage*, you will still be addressing many of the *NLS* objectives when targeting the Early learning goals.

Some professionals working at the Foundation stage, however, feel pressurised to teach towards the goals themselves, and are concerned that the stepping stones become overlooked. It is crucial that all children work at an appropriate level and are not pushed ahead too soon towards future outcomes. As professionals, therefore, we need to stand firm in our approach to working with all children at their own level, in their own time. By recording their achievements and showing why they are working on the current stepping stone, we will be able to illustrate the positive reasons for doing this.

Planned activities and appropriate intervention

A second debate to come out of the *Curriculum guidance for the foundation stage* is the principle it promotes of 'activities planned by adults' and 'appropriate intervention' to help the children in their learning (DfEE 2000: 11). Some practitioners feel that children should be left to learn through play, without any intervention by adults, while others may find themselves heavily directing the children's activities in order to highlight a learning point.

Most practitioners, though, would agree that the ideal is a balance between these two and the skill comes in knowing when and how to intervene, to maximise the children's learning opportunity. Leaving children to play freely in the belief that they will eventually learn the targeted skill or concept through discovery, assumes that learning is a sort of process of osmosis by which knowledge is automatically absorbed. This takes learning through play to a questionable extreme and will end up throwing the baby out with the bathwater – a child can play freely all day long without actually coming around to the learning point that the practitioner is aiming for. On the other hand, intervention can easily become interference – it can stifle children's exuberance and enthusiasm for the activity, because their curiosity and creativity are hampered by too much direction from the adult. This will never lead to effective learning. The practitioner needs to be sensitive as to when and how to intervene in the children's play, to help them discover the learning point.

In her book *Understanding Children's Play* (Nelson Thornes 2001), Jennie Lindon outlines the different roles that the professional plays when interacting with the child, including, for example, play companion, model, mediator, facilitator, observer-learner, etc. If you come to recognise which of these roles is appropriate to adopt in a given situation, you will go a long way to making sure children's learning is positive and successful, and fun. The skill lies in ensuring that structure and intervention are there in your planning, which in turn allows the children to determine the nature of the play.

Working towards literacy

When working to develop children's literacy skills, we need to bear in mind that literacy is not confined to reading and writing. All aspects of language as a whole, including speaking, listening, comprehension, expression and conversational skills, are crucial components of literacy. Without language, literacy skills can't be learnt. Speaking and listening feature largely in the *Curriculum guidance for the foundation stage* and so are acknowledged as the fundamental basis of the acquisition of literacy skills. While self-analysis and consideration of others' opinions are featured as objectives at a later stage of the *National Literacy Strategy*, children in the early years need to be introduced to these concepts. Paying attention to and taking account of others' views is part of the Foundation stage work. Very young children have differing opinions as much as adults and older children, and they need to realise that opinions which are different from their own deserve to be respected and valued.

The reverse of this coin is that they should be able to develop the confidence to express their own opinion in the knowledge that it will be seen as a valuable contribution to the discussions held by the whole group. They must know that even if their opinion is different from others', it is a valid one and will be welcomed by everyone as an alternative view.

Imaginative play, creativity and role-play are also important elements in language development, and therefore in acquiring literacy skills. If we enable children to explore and play in imaginative situations, their ability to understand and enjoy fiction will be enhanced, as will their own creative literary abilities. Fiction and stories are, after all, only a different medium for expressing the creative play that goes on in every early years Home Corner!

Literacy (and language), as such, is not an isolated bubble or a 'subject' of the curriculum to be taught at specific times of the day. It cuts across every area of learning and is part of everything we do. While it is convenient for the sake of record keeping and planning to talk about 'Literacy', it's really something that can't be pigeon-holed or put onto a form with tick-boxes to record when we have 'done' it. It permeates every part of learning: reading the labels on maths equipment together may happen during a maths session, but it's still literacy; writing captions on the bottom of a painting links art and literacy.

So it soon becomes clear how using play, games and fun activities are ways we can approach literacy, enabling the children to develop the skills they need.

Who is this book for?

I hope that all early years practitioners will find something useful in this book and by 'all practitioners', I mean professionals who work in any capacity within the field of early years education. I have tried to use 'neutral' language in the book, i.e. not school-based terms, since the education of early years children takes place in many settings other than schools or nominated educational establishments.

Although I have explored some of the issues involved in the *Curriculum guidance for the foundation stage/National Literacy Strategy* debate, this is not to say the implications are only for schools. I would argue that they affect everyone providing education for young children and so the issues are just as relevant to non-school settings. (However, since the *NLS* phonics programme continues to the end of Year 2, and therefore is included in the daily Literacy Hour, in the chapters covering Years 1 and 2, I have been unable to avoid including some elements that appear to be more structured and formal. I chose to explore the phonics and suggest some activities for these two years because the children are still within the early years stage of education.)

But aside from this, I hope that the book will be useful to practitioners thanks to the practical nature of the ideas and suggestions. The activities can be done either within the framework of a session aiming for one of the official curriculum targets, or as a non-curriculum session with the setting's own aims in view. Of course, the activities are only suggestions, and practitioners could easily adapt or change them to suit their own situation.

What's in the book?

The book covers the elements of phonics, from the basic awareness and discrimination of general and environmental sounds, through awareness and discrimination of the subtleties of body, voice and speech sounds, to the fine-tuning of phoneme awareness, recognition, discrimination and blending. It is crucial that children have skills in all these elements of phonics if they are to develop the literacy abilities necessary for reading and writing. Phonics in all its aspects can be used as the basis of activities that are fun and which contain an element of play, yet still have a literacy skill as the target. In the book, I have used and recommended many of the games and activities featured in *Phonics with CD-ROM, Progression in phonics: materials for whole-class teaching* (DfEE 1999, 2000) (*PiPs*) because they are a fun way of reinforcing a teaching point.

The book has an accompanying CD, which can be used as it stands or recorded from if you find tracks of particular interest for a specific teaching point. It features some tracks that are specifically designed for you as the practitioner, such as the correct pronunciation of all the phonemes, and others that have activities that the children can work on independently, while listening to the CD alone, or together – with you offering support when you think it's needed. In line with my aim in all the books in this series, I have made the CD as a 'pick and mix' resource for you to use as you wish.

There are two observation and assessment sections at the end of the book to give the practitioner an idea of what to look for when the children are working to acquire a specific skill. These sections are by no means exhaustive and practitioners can 'pick and mix' the elements that are most useful to them, adding anything that they may feel needs to be included. I can't stress enough the importance of observation as a tool for assessment, since so much can be gathered of a child's achievements, progress and performance by this simple but extremely effective practice. The stepping stones in the *Curriculum guidance for the foundation stage* can also provide a useful guide to the child's achievements, particularly as the colour bands help to put the stepping stones into an age-related context. But we need to remember that they are just that – a guide to the child's progress en route to the Early learning goals – and not be tempted to use them as an assessment or teaching tool as such.

There are also some photocopiable pages which are linked in with the activities. They are not worksheets to be given to the children to 'do', but are a resource to save the practitioner preparation time. They must be used by the adult and the children working together on the activity, in a fun way without pressure.

What's in a chapter?

Each chapter follows more or less the same format:

- Phonic focus – the particular phoneme or phonic rule being explored.
- Early learning goals from *Curriculum guidance for the foundation stage*, and/or phonics-based objectives from the *National Literacy Strategy*, which link in with the Early learning goals in Chapter 1. Chapters 2 and 3 focus on the relevant objectives from the *National Literacy Strategy* relating to phonics for Years 1 and 2 respectively. Where appropriate, there are reference lists of words related to a specific phoneme – these are to save you the time it takes to plough through a dictionary when you need words to make games cards and so on.
- Materials needed – everything needed to do the session and activities.
- Optional materials for other activities – a list of resources needed for the other structured play activities.
- Preparation – details of what needs to be done beforehand. This often includes something like *Make a set of picture matching cards using Photocopiable Sheet 5*. The most effective way of doing this is to photocopy the sheet, stick it onto card and when the glue is dry, cut the sheet into the individual cards. You might like to ask the children to colour those cards that have pictures. You could laminate the cards for future use and to protect against everyday wear and tear.
- Introducing the phoneme – for you as the practitioner either with everyone together or in groups, as you require. Although this section has been scripted, this is for guidance only and naturally you should present the material in your own 'style'. There may be questions asked and issues explored in this section which you feel aren't appropriate for your

children's achievement level. The flexibility of the session means that you can 'pick and mix' those bits that *are* relevant to your own situation, leaving out what you don't want, or exploring further something that may be looked at in less detail than you'd like. There may be times when you'd prefer to explore a phonic focus together over several sessions and therefore you might only use part of the section each time.

- Focus activities – these can be done in whichever way you prefer, e.g. adult-led, in groups, independent, child-selected, etc. They have been designed to cater for different achievement levels and obviously you should 'pick and mix' as you require. You could adapt, add to or ignore them according to your own setting's needs. Some of the games have a competitive element in them, for example by winning tokens or avoiding 'elimination'. These can be adapted, if you prefer, to leave out that element of the game, in which case the children's satisfaction at their own achievement is the outcome of the activity. Sometimes there are songs to sing in the introductory sessions and/or the focus activities, and these are always with tunes from well-known songs or rhymes. I have followed the excellent example of Sue Nicholls (*Bobby Shaftoe, clap your hands*, A & C Black 1992) by including, in the appropriate place, the first few bars of each tune as a memory-jogger. They appear both as notes to be played on a xylophone and written as the melody. The xylophone notes you will need are:

B, C D E F G A B C' D'

(the comma after the first B indicates low B, and the apostrophes after C and D indicate high C and D).

- Other structured play activities – suggestions for other things to do as an 'optional extra'. They bring in wider aspects of Early learning goals and/or the *NLS* objectives, beyond the chapter's main focus. Some of the activities are competitive but, as mentioned above, you can adapt them to leave out this element, if you prefer.
- Related photocopiable sheets.

CHAPTER 1

Foundation stage and Reception Year

Auditory awareness and auditory discrimination of environmental sounds

Stepping stones from *Curriculum guidance for the foundation stage*, Communication, language and literacy:

- Distinguish one sound from another.
- Use writing as a means of recording and communicating.

Materials needed

- Copy of *Bobby Shaftoe, clap your hands* by Sue Nicholls (A & C Black 1992)
- Flip-chart and marker pens, easel and board, Blutack, card, scissors, glue
- CD player and CD accompanying this book (see 'Preparation')
- Two sets of picture cards to accompany the CD (see 'Preparation')
- Small screen or a box laid on its side, a variety of everyday objects such as water in a bottle and a glass, a cup and saucer, a radio, a ticking clock, paper for screwing up, a handbell, cutlery and so on
- Cassette recorders, blank cassettes (see 'Preparation')
- Selection of toys or models of things that make noises in reality (for example, a car, a bird, a dog, a clock, a kettle and so on), feely bag

Optional materials for other activities

- CD player and CD accompanying this book, with the environmental sounds
- The everyday objects used during the introductory session

Preparation

- ▲ Have the CD player with the CD ready to play at track 1; make two sets of picture cards using Photocopiable Sheets 1 and 2 (pp. 32 and 33): stick the sheets to card and cut them into the individual pictures; fix one set to the easel.
- ▲ Collect the everyday objects and hide them behind the screen or in the box.
- ▲ Put the collection of toys and models into the feely bag.
- ▲ Record on one of the blank cassettes the noises you will make with the everyday objects (for example, rattle the cutlery, play the radio for a few moments and so on), pausing for long enough between each noise to allow the children to switch the player off and on again without losing the next sound; leave the cassette in the player.

Introducing the phonic focus

You might prefer to introduce the phonic focus over more than one session:

- Ask the children to be very quiet for a few moments and listen to the sounds around them. What can they hear? For example, traffic going past, noises coming from the kitchen, other children playing outside and so on. List the children's suggestions on the flip-chart, either by drawing a simple picture or writing a keyword. According to achievement level, the children could do this themselves or you could scribe for them. Ask the children to think about whether the noises they hear are loud or quiet, whether they go on for a long time or a short time, whether the noise is repeated or heard only once.

- Together, sing *Listen, children* from *Bobby Shaftoe, clap your hands* by Sue Nicholls. If you don't have a copy of the book, you could sing the following together to the tune of *Frère Jacques* (see Figure 1.1):

> What can you hear? What can you hear?
> Can you say? Can you say?
> I can hear a . . . , I can hear a . . . ,
> You can too, you can too.

Pause for a moment to listen after *What can you hear? What can you hear?* and then let the children take turns to sing the third line by themselves.

- Play track 1 of the CD, which features the environmental noises and listen to each in turn. Play a game where the children have to put up their hand as soon as they know what the sound is. Invite one of them to point to the relevant picture card on the easel and tell you what the sound was on the CD.
- Tell the children that this time you're going to make some noises and they have to guess what the sounds are. When they think they recognise the sound they should put up their hand. Using the everyday objects you collected, make a sound behind the screen or in the box. For example, screw up the piece of paper, chink the cup and saucer or pour the water from the bottle into the glass. Give the children enough time to listen and decide what the noise is. If they need to hear it again, repeat the action. Make each sound one at a time and ask the children what it could be.
- Play two games: in the first, the children take turns to come out and make one of the noises behind the screen and the others have to guess what it is; in the second, the children each have one of the picture cards that go with this track on the CD, and when you play the sounds, the child holding the matching card has to hold it up as quickly as possible.

Focus activities

Group A: Take the children outside with the cassette recorder and blank cassette. Help them to record some of the sounds they can hear. For example, road works going on nearby, traffic going past, a game of football being played and so on. Have fun back indoors listening to the recording and remembering what it was that made the sounds on the cassette. The children could draw some pictures to illustrate each sound.

Group B: Give the recorded cassette and player to the children. Play a game where they listen to a sound that you have recorded, guess what it is and then mime the action. According to achievement level, they could operate the player by themselves. Remind them they can switch it off between sounds to give them time to guess and then do the miming actions.

Group C: Give the feely bag containing the selection of toys and models to the children. Play a game where they take turns to pick a model or toy from the feely bag and then try to copy the noise it would make, using their voices. For example, if they took out a car, they might say *brrrrrrrmmmmmmmmm* or if they picked a cow, they may say *mmmmmooooooooooooo*.

Group D: Put a set of the picture cards that accompany the CD face down on the table. Let the children play a game where they take turns to pick a card, look at the picture and name it. They should then use their voices to try to make the noise that they would hear the real object making.

Group E: Place the picture cards that accompany the CD track 1 face up on the table. Play a game where you listen to the sounds on the CD and the first child to point to the correct card can hold it. The winner is the person with the most cards at the end of the game.

Other structured play activities

- Let the children listen to the CD and have fun naming the noises and/or matching them with the accompanying picture cards.
- Let the children play freely with the everyday objects behind the screen, which were used in the introductory session. Encourage them to explore the noises they make.
- Let the children have fun recording voice noises onto a cassette using pictures from magazines and books in the Library Corner as a stimulus. For example, they could say *sssssssssss* for the picture of a snake or *vrrrrroooommmmmm* for a motor bike.

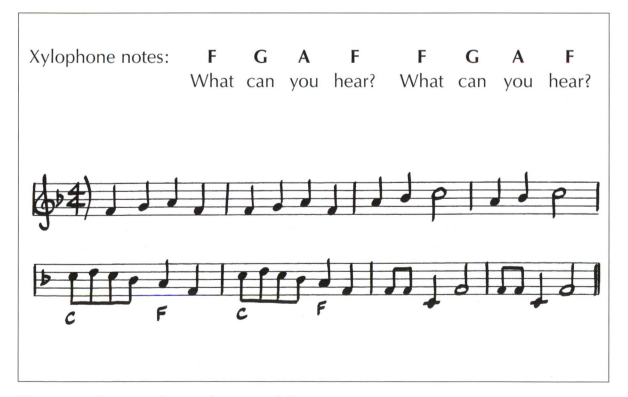

Figure 1.1 Sing together to the tune of *Frère Jacques*

PHONIC FOCUS

Auditory awareness and auditory discrimination of instrumental sounds

Stepping stones from *Curriculum guidance for the foundation stage*, Communication, language and literacy:

- Distinguish one sound from another.
- Use writing as a means of recording and communicating.

Materials needed

- A selection of musical instruments, if possible two of each (e.g. shakers, Indian bells, castanets, tambourines, small drums, triangles, whistles and so on. You might prefer to use only two instruments at first if the children find difficulty in discriminating between them, and adding more to the collection as the children find the games easier.)
- A screen or a box
- CD player and CD accompanying this book (see 'Preparation')
- Instrument cards (see 'Preparation')
- Cassette recorder, blank cassette
- *Bobby Shaftoe, clap your hands* by Sue Nicholls (A & C Black 1992)

Optional materials for other activities

- CD player and CD accompanying this book (see 'Preparation')
- *Bobby Shaftoe, clap your hands* by Sue Nicholls (A & C Black 1992)
- A selection of musical instruments
- Junk for making musical instruments (e.g. small empty boxes, cardboard tubes, rubber bands, etc.). (Make sure none of the children is allergic to the junk items themselves or to what they originally contained.)

Preparation

- ▲ Put one of each pair of the instruments behind the screen or in the box; have the others accessible to the children.
- ▲ Have the CD player with the CD ready to play at track 2.
- ▲ Make a set of cards each with the picture of one instrument used during the introductory session; put a set of the instruments behind the screen, for Group B.
- ▲ Make a set of cards with 'loud', 'quiet', 'fast' or 'slow' written on each one. Put the blank cassette into the recorder and leave them ready for the children to make a recording.

Introducing the phonic focus

You might prefer to introduce the phonic focus over more than one session:

- Together, explore the instruments and let the children experiment by handling and playing them freely – they need to be familiar with the sounds made by each instrument before playing the games. Help them to identify each instrument by name – you could do this by asking the children to place each one in front of the screen. For example, 'Harvinder, put the shaker on the table, please'.

- Let the children play a guessing game with the instruments. One child goes behind the screen and plays an instrument, and the others have to guess which one it is – you might prefer to use only two instruments at first, adding more as the children become better at the game. (If the children have forgotten the name of the instrument, let them point to the duplicate in front of the screen.) The first child to guess which instrument was played then takes a turn at playing a different one behind the screen, for the others to guess.

- Ask different children to come up and play an instrument, either by name or by characteristic. For example, 'Michael, come and play the whistle' or 'Leon, come and play something you can hit' (a triangle, a drum, a cymbal or a tambourine, etc.). Have fun by asking the children to play some of the instruments loudly, quietly, quickly or slowly. Let the others guess how the instrument is being played – the child who guesses correctly can play the next round.

- Listen to the instruments being played on the CD (tracks 2 and 3) and ask the children to tell you whether they are being played loudly, quietly, quickly or slowly. Let them copy the CD by playing the instruments in the same way – play the example on the CD first and then ask the children to 'echo' it. If the children are ready, you could challenge them to play their instruments loudly and quickly, quietly and slowly, loudly and slowly or quietly and quickly.

Focus activities

You may decide to do these at different times, as several groups simultaneously doing different musical activities can be quite a challenge to the ears!:

Group A: Sing a song to the tune of *Tommy Thumb* (see Figure 1.2), naming different instruments and with different children playing the named instrument when they sing 'Here I am'. For example, 'Tambourine, tambourine, where are you?' and Suzie plays the tambourine while everyone sings 'Here I am, here I am. How do you do?' (Don't worry about rhythm here – the main aim is to recognise the instrument and become familiar with its sound.)

Group B: Put the instrument cards on the table so that the children can see the pictures clearly. Start the game by playing one of the instruments. The child who points to the correct card then takes the next turn to play an instrument.

Group C: Give the children the cassette recorder and blank cassette, and put the 'loud', 'quiet', 'fast' and 'slow' cards face down on the table. Let each child choose an instrument and then play a game where they take a card and play their instrument according to the instruction. (You may need to help them read their card.) Record the children as they play so that they can play matching games and/or listen to themselves later.

Group D: Play some instruments to the tune of *Baa Baa Black Sheep* (see Figure 1.3), focusing on loudly, quietly, quickly and/or slowly, as you wish. For example,

> *Listen, listen, can you hear us play?*
> *Loudly, loudly (quietly/quickly/slowly), here we go;*
> *James plays the tambourine (shaker etc.), Luke plays the bells (drum etc.);*
> *Loudly, loudly, can you hear?*

Group E: Play a game by singing *One sound can be heard* from *Bobby Shaftoe, clap your hands* by Sue Nicholls. Use the instruments from the introductory session and, according to achievement level, add some more.

Other structured play activities

- Let the children listen to the CD to play copying and/or matching games freely with the instruments.
- Play *Musical box* from *Bobby Shaftoe, clap your hands* by Sue Nicholls.
- Help the children to make some new instruments for the collection. When they are finished, have fun playing some of the games from the earlier sessions.
- Take the children and the instruments outside and let them explore how the sounds made by the instruments are different. For example, a triangle will be more difficult to hear when traffic is passing, a drum won't have quite the same effect in a playground, and so on.

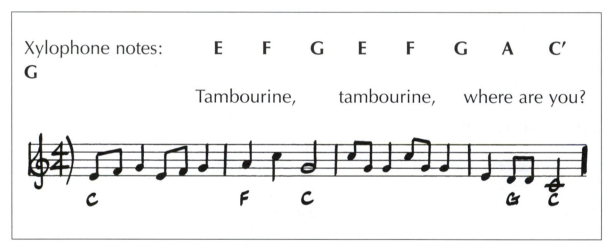

Figure 1.2 Sing together to the tune of *Tommy Thumb*

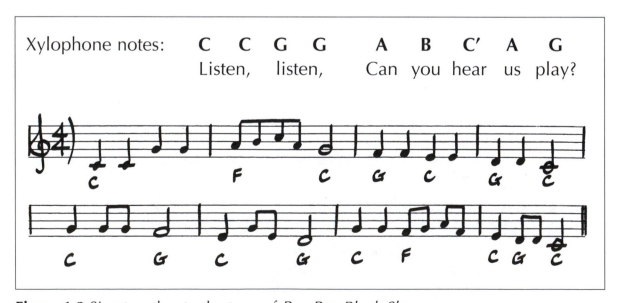

Figure 1.3 Sing together to the tune of *Baa Baa Black Sheep*

PHONIC FOCUS

Auditory awareness and auditory discrimination of body sounds

Stepping stones from *Curriculum guidance for the foundation stage*, Communication, language and literacy:

- Distinguish one sound from another.
- Use writing as a means of recording and communicating.

Materials needed

- A screen big enough for the children to hide behind
- Flip-chart and marker pens
- Body part cards (see 'Preparation'), card, scissors, glue
- CD player and CD accompanying this book
- Cassette recorder/player and blank cassette (see 'Preparation')

Optional materials for other activities

- *Bobby Shaftoe, clap your hands* by Sue Nicholls (A & C Black 1992)

Preparation

- ▲ Using Photocopiable Sheets 3 and 4 (pp. 34 and 35) make two sets of body part cards by sticking the sheets on card and cutting them into the individual cards.
- ▲ Record onto the cassette some action songs such as: *Heads, shoulders, knees and toes; This is the way we clap our hands (Here we go round the mulberry bush); If you're happy and you know it; Peter taps with one hammer* and so on. Don't use any instruments to accompany your singing – you want the children to concentrate on sounds and actions made by their bodies.

Introducing the phonic focus

- Let the children choose a favourite nursery rhyme and recite it together, keeping the beat or rhythm with body percussion (for example, by clapping or tapping etc.):

Jack and Jill went **up** the hill	(clap hands twice)
To **fetch** a pail of **water**;	(click fingers twice)
Jack fell down and **broke** his crown	(tap head twice)
And **Jill** came tumbling **after**.	(clap hands twice)

- Together, explore the different ways of making body sounds and spend some time listening to each one, so the children become familiar with them. Some ways to make body sounds are: clapping hands; tapping with two fingers on the palm of the other hand; patting knees, thighs or calves with a flattened hand; knocking knuckles together; tapping the head with knuckles; knocking the chest with knuckles or a flattened hand; patting cheeks with the mouth opened or closed; experimenting with different breathing noises through the nose or the mouth; stamping feet; knocking feet together; tapping toes on the floor; and drumming nails on the table. Some children can become very excited doing these, so encourage them to do the actions gently in order to hear the sounds they make.

- When you are happy that the children are confident in identifying and discriminating the different body sounds, play a guessing game with them. Ask one child to go behind the screen to make a body percussion sound. Sing the following to the tune of *Hickory Dickory Dock* (see Figure 1.4):

> *Listen to Stephanie (Benny, Amil, etc.) play,*
> *Listen to Stephanie play,*
> *Can you hear? Can you hear?*
> *Tell us what Stephanie plays.*

Then Stephanie makes her body sound and the child who guesses it correctly is the next person to go behind the screen. You could challenge the children to try guessing two body sounds performed in the same 'go'!

- Have some fun experimenting with tempo and volume while doing the body percussion sounds. For example, clapping slowly and loudly, tapping quickly and quietly, stamping loudly and quickly or rubbing palms quietly and slowly. Let one child do the body percussion sounds and ask the others to tell you how they were played. Initially, it's probably best to do this with the others seeing the player. If the children are confident at naming the actions, then the player could go behind the screen to give the others an extra challenge.

Focus activities

Group A: Get the group to sit in a circle. One child starts off by doing some body percussion, repeating the action until everyone has joined in. (If the child can't think of an action to do, you may have to help by suggesting one.) The others should copy the leader as soon as they can. When the whole group is playing the body percussion together, change the leader and begin again.

Group B: Help the children to compose some music using body percussion. Let each child choose a body sound to perform and then let the group decide on the best way to put together all the sounds, to create the final version. Choose a simple diagram for each child's idea and write the 'notation' on the flip-chart. If you prefer, you could work with the children to make a shorter piece by deciding together on fewer body sounds and learning those. When they are ready, record their composition on a cassette for the others to listen to.

Group C: Put the body part cards on the table face down in two piles. Play a game where the children take two cards and try to make a body percussion action to include the body parts shown on the cards. For example, if they pick a hand card and an elbow card, they could tap one elbow with the opposite hand. (If the children pick cards that don't work such as a head and a shoulder, just let them pick the next card off the pile, after they have discovered that the original choice won't work.)

Group D: Help the children to listen to the accompanying CD (track 4), which gives instructions for making different body percussion sounds. Let them choose their favourite(s) to practise and learn.

Group E: Give the cassette player and recorded cassette to the children and let them listen to the songs and join in. Encourage them to perform the actions as they sing.

Other structured play activities

- Play *Clap hands, follow me* from *Bobby Shaftoe, clap your hands* by Sue Nicholls. Let the children make up the body percussion actions, singing a verse for each child.
- Let the children experiment with designing some simple pictures to illustrate some of their favourite body percussion actions. Give them some marker pens and encourage them to try out their ideas on the flip-chart. Remind them that they can change their minds and start again if they don't like their first attempts.
- Let the children listen to the accompanying CD (track 4), which gives instructions for making different body percussion sounds. Let them choose their favourite(s) to practise and learn.

(Note: For more ideas about using body percussion, see *Clap Hands* by Denise Bailey in *Nursery World*, 11 July 2002.)

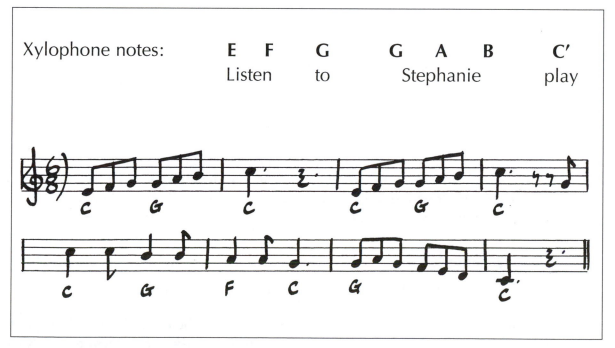

Figure 1.4 Sing together to the tune of *Hickory Dickory Dock*

Auditory awareness and auditory discrimination of speech and voice sounds

Stepping stones from *Curriculum guidance for the foundation stage*, Communication, language and literacy:

- Distinguish one sound from another.
- Use writing as a means of recording and communicating.

Materials needed

- Screen large enough for the children to hide behind, speaker-selection cards and feely bag (optional – see 'Preparation'), feeling/face picture cards (see 'Preparation'), card, scissors, glue, flip-chart and marker pens
- CD player and CD accompanying this book
- Group-sound cards (see 'Preparation')
- A selection of junk items to experiment with voice sounds. For example, empty yoghurt cartons, cardboard tubes, tissue and comb, and so on. (Make sure none of the children is allergic to the junk itself or anything that was originally in the containers.)

Optional materials for other activities

- Cassette recorder/player and blank cassette

Preparation

- ▲ If you don't have another adult to go with the children behind the screen, you could make speaker-selection cards to select a speaker. Make sure that there's one for each child and that these are all blank except for one, which should have a tick mark drawn on it. Put the cards into a feely bag and the child who takes out the marked card will be the speaker in the guessing game.
- ▲ Make a set of feeling/face picture cards using Photocopiable Sheets 5 and 6 (pp. 36 and 37): stick the sheets onto card and cut them into the individual picture cards.
- ▲ Familiarise yourself with tracks 5 and 6 of the CD accompanying this book.
- ▲ Make a set of group-sound cards using Photocopiable Sheets 7–10 (pp. 38–41).

Introducing the phonic focus

You may decide to introduce the phonic focus over more than one session:

- Tell the children you're all going to play a guessing game where they have to listen very carefully. Send three or four children behind the screen and ask one of them to say, 'Can you guess who I am?' Encourage the rest of the children to guess who is speaking. If they need to hear the voice again, ask the speaker behind the screen to repeat the question. (Remember not to inadvertently say the speaker's name!) Have several goes at the game, changing the small group of children behind the screen each time.

- Have some fun with the feeling/face picture cards, making up voice sounds to express the mood of each picture. For example, the children might say 'Aaaaahhhhh' for the *afraid* card or 'oohhhhhhhhhh' for the *disappointed* card. Spend a bit of time talking about how our voices change with each feeling we express. Can the children think of other feelings and some voice sounds to go with them? Use the flip-chart to draw simple face pictures and write the suggested voice sounds (spelt phonetically), to record the children's ideas.
- Help the children to focus on the different tones and frequencies that their voices can express. Give them stimulus words such as 'squeak', 'growl', 'shout', 'whisper', 'hum', 'loud', 'quiet' and so on. Let them experiment with these sounds and enjoy using their voices freely. When they are ready, encourage them to make up voice sounds for different scenarios. For example, if they're really angry about someone who broke their favourite toy or if they have a pain in their tummy (see Figure 1.5).
- Listen to track 5 of the CD accompanying this book and have fun with the children guessing what could be making each noise. For example, do they guess that *Wheeeeeeeee* could mean going down a slide?

Focus activities

Group A: Let the children listen to track 5 of the CD and try to guess why the 'speaker' makes each sound. Encourage them to copy the sound themselves. Let them play a game where one child imitates a sound from the CD and the others have to guess what the sound might illustrate.

Group B: Give the feeling/face picture cards to the children and let them have fun making up voice sounds to express each one. They could play a game where the cards are placed face down and the children take turns to pick one. Without showing the pictures to others, they should make a voice sound to express the feeling and the others should guess what it is.

Group C: Give the children the group-sound cards and let them make up voice sounds for each one. When they have decided on their sounds, help them to record these onto a cassette. They can listen to the cassette later, or record different sounds if they wish.

Group D: Listen to track 6 of the CD with the children and help them to make up a voice sound to go with each 'scenario'. Help them to discover that there may be more than one way of expressing the situation. If you give them the CD to play by themselves, remind them to switch off the player when the voice tells them to.

Group E: Give the children a selection of junk items and let them experiment with making voice sounds. For example, let them buzz on a comb and tissue paper, hum into an empty yoghurt carton, whistle into a plastic funnel or speak down a card cone. Help them to record their experimental noises onto a cassette.

Other structured play activities

- Play a game of Chinese whispers using one of the voice sounds as the message.
- Go outside and encourage the children to try out their voice sounds. What happens when an aeroplane flies overhead or if there are roadworks nearby?

- Let the children record onto a cassette as many different voice sounds as they can. Encourage them to think about using their lips, teeth, breath, tongue and cheeks to make different noises. When they have finished, they can listen to their recording and practise the sounds, or add some more.

(Note: Some recommended texts for exploring voice sounds and body percussion are *Noisy Farm* by Rod Campbell (Puffin 1994), *We're Going on a Bear Hunt* by Michael Rosen (Walker Books 1993), *Cock a Moo Moo* by Juliet Dallas-Conte (Macmillan 2001) and *Peace at Last* by Jill Murphy (Macmillan 1995).)

---

1. You have a pain in your tummy.
2. You're really angry because someone broke your favourite toy.
3. You're very, very tired.
4. Something suddenly gives you a big fright.
5. You're going to be in trouble with your mummy in a minute.
6. You're very hot.
7. You're pretending to be a monkey.
8. You're whizzing down a slide very fast.
9. You're feeling very cold.
10. You're really disappointed about something.

Figure 1.5 Scenarios for experimenting with voice sounds

PHONIC FOCUS

Rhythm, rhyme and alliteration

Stepping stones from *Curriculum guidance for the foundation stage*, Communication, language and literacy:

- Distinguish one sound from another.
- Show awareness of rhyme...
- Show awareness of...alliteration.
- Hear and say initial sounds in words and know which letters represent some of the sounds.
- Use writing as a means of recording and communicating.

Objectives from the *National Literacy Strategy (YR)*:

- To hear and identify initial sounds in words.
- To identify alliteration in known and new and invented words.
- To sound and name each letter of the alphabet in lower and upper case.
- To write letters in response to letter names.

Materials needed

- Big book of nursery or other familiar rhymes (practitioner's own choice)
- Tambourine or drum (optional)
- A peg, a hat, a tin and a feely bag
- Flip-chart and marker pens
- Poem *One Wonderful Worm* (see 'Preparation')
- *Progression in phonics: materials for whole-class teaching* (DfEE 1999, 2000)
- The children's name cards, a selection of musical instruments
- Triangles of paper, pens or markers, string
- Picture/word cards (see 'Preparation'), card, scissors, glue
- Theme picture cards (e.g. fruit and vegetable, animals, vehicles, etc.)

Optional materials for other activities

- CD player and CD accompanying this book
- Cassette recorder/player and blank cassette (optional)
- Card, marker pens, paper, pencils

Preparation

- ▲ Put the peg, hat and tin into the feely bag.
- ▲ Enlarge *One Wonderful Worm* (see Figure 1.7).
- ▲ Make a set of picture/word cards using Photocopiable Sheet 11 (p. 42): stick the sheet to card and cut it into the individual pictures.
- ▲ Familiarise yourself with tracks 7, 8 and 9 of the CD.

Introducing the phonic focus

You might prefer to introduce the phonic focus over more than one session:

- **(Rhythm)** Together, share some of the rhymes from the big book to discover their rhythms. Let the children choose which rhymes to sing and recite them as a group, encouraging the children to move to the rhythm. For example, they could rock gently back and forth to *Rockabye Baby* or *Bye Baby Bunting*, or they could jig up and down to *To market, to market to buy a fat pig*. If you have the room, you could encourage them to march in time to *The Grand Old Duke of York* or *Little Boy Blue*.
- When you have explored the rhythms of two or three rhymes, tell the children you're going to clap the rhythm of one, and they should listen carefully. Can they guess which rhyme you are clapping? Encourage them to join in the clapping for a few moments, then add the words and recite the rhyme together once again.
- Have some fun clapping the rhythm of the children's names – for a different experience they could use the tambourine or drum instead of clapping. Sing together to the tune of *Baa Baa Black Sheep*, like this:

> *Susan, Susan (James/Pritpal, etc.), can you clap (tap) your name?*
> *Yes, sir; yes, sir; yes you can.*

(The named child taps his or her name before the others continue singing.)

> *You clapped your name for us, we know;*
> *Now we can all do it and this is how it goes:*

(All the children then clap or tap the name together.)

- **(Rhyme)** Tell the children that now you're all going to play a rhyming game using the little things in the feely bag. Ask a volunteer to take out one of the objects and tell you what it is before passing it to the next child, who should say a word that rhymes with the name, and then pass it on again. Tell the children that nonsense words are allowed. For example, if the peg is taken out of the bag, the next words could be *leg, feg, beg, neg* and so on. Repeat the game until all three objects have been used. According to achievement level, you could write the beginning of each rhyming chain on the flip-chart and invite the children to add to it by following the pattern.
- Once the children are confident in making rhyming chains, have some fun playing with traditional or familiar rhymes by changing some of the words and encouraging the children to supply alternatives. For example,

> *Baa Baa Black Sheep, have you got a hat?*
> *Yes, sir; yes, sir; and a black . . . (bat/cat/mat/rat).*

(For more examples, see Figure 1.6.) According to achievement level, you could write the new rhymes on the flip-chart and leave them up for the children to read and recite in their own time.

- **(Alliteration)** Say to the children some of the alliterative sentences from *Progression in phonics: materials for whole-class teaching*. (Use expression, tempo and tone to make them sound interesting.) After each one, ask the children what they notice about the words. Repeat the sentences, encouraging the children to join in and enjoy the feel of the words on their tongues.

- Share some tongue-twisters such as *Peter Piper picked a peck of pickled pepper* and *Around the rugged rock the ragged rascal ran*. Can the children tell you the repeated phonemes in each one? Read the poem *One Wonderful Worm* (Figure 1.7) to the children, tracking the words with your finger as you read. Spend a bit of time exploring the poem together, encouraging the children to discover the alliteration in each line. Read it together once more, with the children joining in.
- Can the children think of some alliterative phrases of their own? You could give them the first two words to start them off. For example, *One old wobbly...*, *two tall...and three thin...* Have some fun thinking up other examples using the children's names: 'Marvellous Michael', 'Amazing Amil' or 'Super Suzie'. (Make sure they're positive phrases and that the children you choose don't mind.)

Focus activities

Group A: Give the children their name cards and let them choose a musical instrument to play. Let the children have fun playing the rhythm of their names on their instruments. When they are confident with their own names, let them practise playing each other's names as well.

Group B: Continue to play the game from the introductory session where the rhythm of a favourite rhyme is clapped and the children have to guess which rhyme it is. Let the children do the clapping in turn, while the others do the guessing. You may have to help them a little with working out the rhythm of their chosen rhyme.

Group C: Give the children a 'kick-off' word for a rhyming chain. For example, *hat, pin* or *ten*. Encourage them to make a chain as long as possible by saying all the rhyming words they can think of, including nonsense words. List their words on the flip-chart or let them write the words themselves, according to achievement level. Give each child a triangle of paper on which to draw and/or write one of the words from the rhyming chain. Thread the triangles of paper together on a long string and hang it across the room.

Group D: Play a game with the picture/word cards. Put them face down on the table and let the children turn them over one at a time. They should look at the picture and say the word, before chanting *This is a...and it can say...* Each child adds a word that rhymes with the word on the card. Nonsense words are allowed. For example, if they turn over the card with a hen on it, they could chant, *This is a hen and it can say 'ten'*, ('men'/'sen'/'pen'/'gen') and so on.

Group E: Together, use the theme picture cards to make up some alliterative phrases. For example, fruit and vegetable cards could give *brown bananas, chocolate cherries, purple pears, crunchy cabbage, crispy carrots* and so on.

Group F: Help the children to make some alliterative phrases using words beginning with their own initials. For example, David could make up *Daddy's dirty ducks* or *Dogs drink dreadfully*.

Other structured play activities

- Let the children listen to the CD accompanying this book (track 7) and join in reciting the rhymes and/or clapping their rhythms.

- Let the children listen to track 8 of the CD accompanying this book at their own pace, to make up some rhyming chains. They could record onto a cassette all the words they add to their chains.
- Let the children listen to track 9 of the CD accompanying this book and join in reciting the alliterative poem *One Wonderful Worm*.
- Make some cards with the names of colours and adjectives written on them – one word for each card – such as *green, red, sad, angry*, etc. Play a game with the children where they have to pick a card and try to make an alliterative phrase using it, such as *A green goat*.
- Help the children to make up some alliterative phrases with their own names. For example, *Happy Harry, Cheerful Charlie, Super Surinder* and *Terrific Tina*. Let the children write and illustrate their phrases.

---

1. Humpty Dumpty sat on a stool,
    Humpty Dumpty fell in a . . . (pool);
    All the King's horses and all the King's men
    Couldn't pull Humpty from the water again.

2. Oh the Grand Old Duke of York,
    He had ten thousand cats;
    He marched them up to the top of the hill
    While they were wearing . . . (hats).

3. Sing a song of sixpence, a pocket full of sweets;
    Four and twenty blackbirds sitting in their . . . (seats);
    When the seats were shaky, the birds began to shout,
    'We don't want to stay in here so now we're going . . . (out).

4. Jack and Jill went up the hill
    To fetch their Mum a pen;
    Jack fell down and broke his crown,
    He won't do that . . . (again).

5. Hickory dickory dares;
    The mouse ran up the . . . (stairs);
    The stairs were brown, the mouse ran . . . (down)
    Hickory dickory dares.

Figure 1.6 Alternative rhymes with missing words

One Wonderful Worm

Anonymous

One wonderful worm
Two tootling trumpets
Three thumping thunders
Four fat farmers
Five funny fools
Six sizzling sausages
Seven scrumptious stews
Eight elegant elephants
Nine neon numbers
Ten terrifying tigers
Are coming your way!

Figure 1.7 An alliterative poem to recite

Single phonemes *a–z*, *ch*, *sh* and *th*

Early learning goals from *Curriculum guidance for the foundation stage*, Communication, language and literacy:

- Hear and say initial and final sounds in words, and short vowel sounds within words.
- Link sounds to letters, naming and sounding the letters of the alphabet.
- Use their phonic knowledge to write simple regular words and make phonetically plausible attempts at more complex words.
- Explore and experiment with sounds, words and texts.

Objectives from the *National Literacy Strategy (YR)*:

- To hear and identify initial sounds in words.
- To read letter(s) that represent(s) the sound(s): *a–z*, *ch*, *sh*, *th*.
- To write each letter in response to each sound: *a–z*, *ch*, *sh*, *th*.
- To sound and name each letter of the alphabet in lower and upper case.

Materials needed

- ■ CD player and CD accompanying this book
- ■ Flip-chart and marker pens
- ■ Picture cards that illustrate the focus phoneme (see 'Preparation')
- ■ Word slides and/or word circles, as required (see 'Preparation')
- ■ A glove puppet of your choice
- ■ A collection of objects, some beginning with the focus phoneme and some not, a feely bag

Optional materials for other activities

- ■ *Progression in phonics: materials for whole-class teaching* (DfEE 1999, 2000)
- ■ Art, craft and modelling materials
- ■ Alphabet cards

Preparation

- ▲ Familiarise yourself with the correct pronunciation of each phoneme by listening to track 10 of the CD accompanying this book.
- ▲ Make or have ready a set of picture cards that illustrate the focus phoneme.
- ▲ Make word/picture slides and/or word circles, as required (see Figures 1.8 and 1.9).
- ▲ Put the collection of objects into the feely bag.

Introducing the phonemes

This is a general session that can be used for any phoneme:

- Draw or fix onto the flip-chart a large picture of something that begins with the focus phoneme. Does anyone know what sound the picture begins with? Explain to the children that the correct word for 'sound' is 'phoneme'. (Children enjoy using technical terms and it is important that they become familiar with and confident in using the terms used in the literacy curricula.)
- Show the children the formation of the letter for the focus phoneme by writing it on the flip-chart. Talk about the formation as you scribe and then ask the children to practise the formation in the air with their fingers. Make sure they start in the correct place. Ask some of the children to come and write the letter on the flip-chart, encouraging them to say the phoneme aloud as they write. Can the children tell you words they know which begin with that phoneme? Have fun making as long a list as possible, writing their suggestions on the flip-chart. Tell the children you'll leave the list up and they can add to it by themselves later.
- Tell the children you're all going to play the 'Word-clapping game'. The children are allowed to say nonsense words provided the initial phoneme is correct and they're also allowed to 'pass' if they're stuck. Sit in a circle and start a slow handclap. Once the rhythm has been established, say three or four words beginning with the focus phoneme, then point to one of the children who adds an additional word. The next child then says a different word, and so on until everyone has had a go, all the time keeping the rhythmic slow handclap going.
- Play a game of 'Phoneme Football'. Divide the children into two football teams (let the children choose which ones). Ask the children in turn whether a word and/or picture begins with the focus phoneme. For example, *Amal, does 'dog' begin with 'd'?* or *Daisy, does 'man' begin with 'd'?* If their answer is correct, they score a goal. The team that scores the highest number of goals is the winner. You could play a variation of the game by asking about the final phoneme. For example, *Andrew, does 'cat' end with 't'?* or *Yuk Fong, does 'peg' end with 't'?*

Focus activities

Group A: Give the children the picture cards illustrating the focus phoneme. Let them play a game where they have to take a card and describe the object on the picture without naming it. The others have to guess what it is, remembering that its initial phoneme is the focus phoneme from the introductory session. The correct 'guesser' takes the next turn.

Group B: Play a game of 'I hear with my little ear, something beginning with . . .', using the focus phoneme as the clue. Ask each child to say a word – nonsense words are allowed and the children are allowed to 'pass' if they wish – and accept any word that has the correct initial phoneme. You could initially help them in their choice of words by giving them cards with the word and/or a picture on them.

Group C: Help the children to make word/picture slides (or word circles, as required) with words or pictures that begin or end with the focus phoneme, as required. According to achievement level, help them to explore the relevant section of a simple dictionary for the words.

Group D: Play a game with the glove puppet. Start off the game by wearing the puppet and saying 'My name is ... (give a name beginning with the focus phoneme) and in my cupboard I have a ... ', naming something beginning with the focus phoneme. Pass the puppet to all of the children in turn, asking them to copy you but to name a different thing. Allow nonsense words if any of them finds it difficult – the important thing is that they know the focus phoneme.

Group E: Play a game with the objects in the feely bag. Tell the children you're going to show them the items one at a time and they should say the focus phoneme when they see an object beginning with it. Remind them that not everything in the feely bag begins with the phoneme you're working on.

Other structured play activities

- Play some of the games featured in *Progression in phonics: materials for whole-class teaching* (DfEE 1999, 2000: 18–33).
- Make a phoneme zoo with animals that begin with the focus phoneme(s). You could either make it as a frieze or with 3D models. The children could make up some of their own animals. Encourage them to write labels, captions and/or sentence(s) for the display.
- Play 'Grandma Went to Market' where Grandma buys things that all begin or end with the focus phoneme.
- Make a spinning top (see Figure 3.3 on p. 81) with a phoneme on each face. Play a game where the children take turns to spin the top and read the phoneme, give a word beginning or ending with the phoneme and/or say and/or write a sentence that includes the words. Tailor the game according to the children's achievement level.
- Make a table display of objects (brought from home by the children, with permission) that begin with the focus phoneme.
- Make 'phoneme mobiles' with large letters. Ask the children to draw and/or label things beginning with the focus phoneme to add to the mobiles.
- Play 'Treasure Hunt' where you challenge the children to find objects in the room beginning and/or ending with the focus phoneme(s).
- Give the children magazines and catalogues and get them to cut out pictures of things beginning or ending in the focus phoneme. Let them make collages with their pictures and label them.
- Ask the children to make the focus phoneme from a variety of materials such as pasta, play dough or plasticine, sandpaper, dried pulses and so on.
- Give the children a set of alphabet cards, placed face down in a pile on the table. Let them play a game where they turn over a card, read the phoneme and then find or name an object in the room beginning with that phoneme.

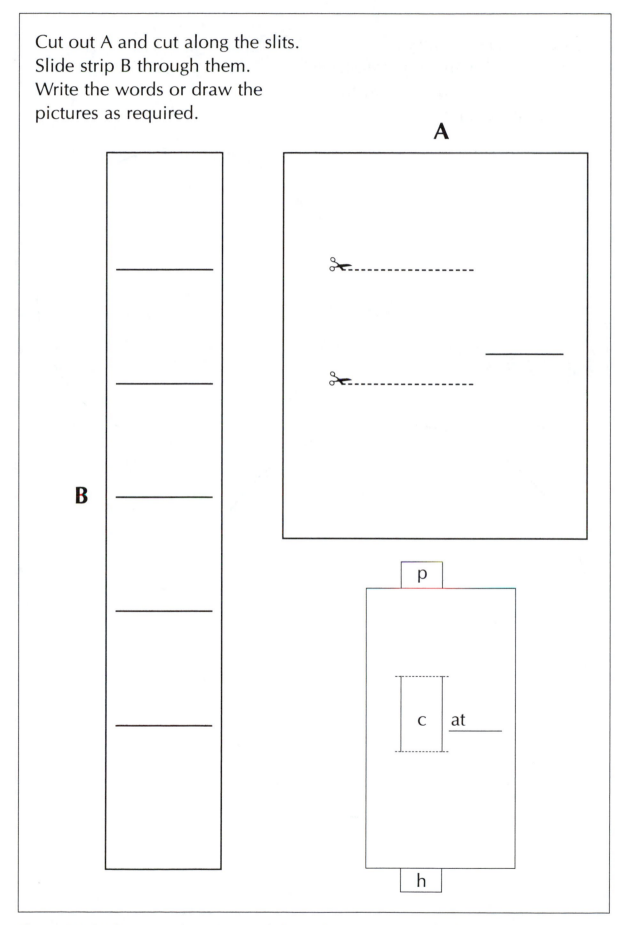

Figure 1.8 Make a word or picture slide as shown to practise a focus phoneme

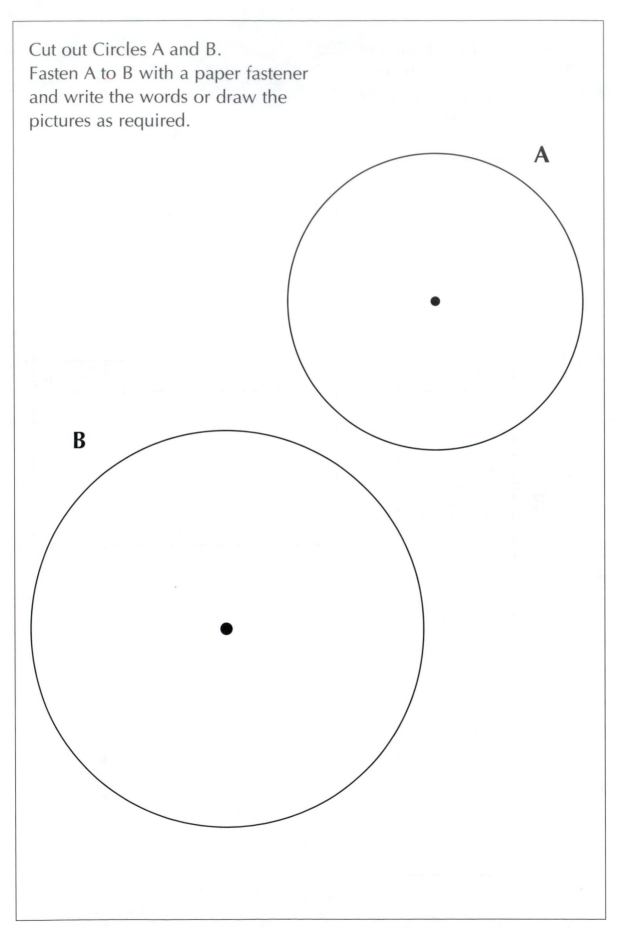

Figure 1.9 Make a word circle as shown here

PHONIC FOCUS

CVC words, onset and rime

(Note: Onset and rime are not addressed in the *Curriculum guidance for the foundation stage*, so you may prefer to leave out those particular sections if you are using only the foundation stage curriculum.)

Early learning goals from *Curriculum guidance for the foundation stage*, Communication, language and literacy:

- Hear and say initial and final sounds in words, and short vowel sounds within words.
- Link sounds to letters, naming and sounding the letters of the alphabet.
- Use their phonic knowledge to write simple regular words and make phonetically plausible attempts at more complex words.
- Explore and experiment with sounds, words and texts.

Objectives from the *National Literacy Strategy (YR)*:

- To identify and write initial and dominant phonemes in spoken words.
- To identify and write initial and dominant phonemes in consonant-vowel-consonant (CVC) words.
- To use knowledge of rhyme to identify families of rhyming CVC words.
- To discriminate 'onsets' from 'rimes' in speech and spelling.

Materials needed

- ■ Flip-chart and different coloured marker pens, a collection of objects with CVC names, a box or feely bag, magnetic board with magnetic letters and three feely bags (see 'Preparation')
- ■ CVC picture cards (see 'Preparation'), magnetic boards and letters, Blutack
- ■ Nursery rhyme book, yellow, white and black paper, pencils or marker pens, glue
- ■ CD player and CD accompanying this book

Optional materials for other activities

- ■ Old newspapers, glue, scissors, white or yellow paper
- ■ Duplicate CVC cards
- ■ Vowel cards, stopwatch or egg timer
- ■ Fishing-rods with magnets on the end, a pond, blend or cluster fish cards (see Chapter 2, 'Preparation', p. 62), card, paper-clips

Preparation

- ▲ Familiarise yourself with the meanings of 'onset' and 'rime'. The beginning phoneme, i.e. consonant or consonant cluster, of a word is its onset. For example, *cat, cot* and *cut* all have the onset **c**; *grapes, grab* and *grunt* all have the onset **gr**; *strap, straight* and *strong* all have the onset **str**. The final syllable, i.e. the last vowel plus consonant or consonant cluster, of a word is its rime. For example, *bin*, *chin* and *grin* all have the rime **in**; *bump*, *jump* and *lump* all have the rime **ump**; *first* and *thirst* both have the rime **irst**. It is important to remember that two rimes don't necessarily rhyme – see the onset examples with non-rhyming rimes of **-apes**, **-ab** and **-unt** – although it's helpful to use rhyming rimes with early years children in order to put across the teaching point.

▲ Put the CVC objects into the box or feely bag; put the magnetic letters into the three feely bags, making sure all the vowels are in one bag, with a selection of consonants in the other two.

▲ Write on the flip-chart (second page) some words that have the same onset but a different rime, e.g. *cap*, *can*, *cat*, *cash* and *catch*.

▲ Write on the flip-chart (third page) some words that have the same rime but a different onset, e.g. *cat*, *hat*, *mat*, *pat*, *flat*, *that* and *chat*.

▲ Make two sets of CVC cards using Photocopiable Sheets 12 and 13 (pp. 43 and 44) (Groups A and B); make sure that the magnetic letters will make the words corresponding to the CVC cards (Group A).

Introducing the phonic focus

You may prefer to introduce the phonic focus over more than one session:

• Play a game with the children where they take an object out of the box or feely bag and tell you its name. Can they tell you the initial, middle and final phonemes? Write the phonemes on the flip-chart, asking the children to tell you what to write. Talk about the vowels in some of the words, using the term *vowels*. Can anyone point to vowels in some of the other words? Can they tell you the phonemes? Challenge them to tell you other words with the same medial vowels.

• Have some fun with tracks 11 and 12 of the CD accompanying this book. Ask the children to listen to the instructions and answer as quickly as they can. Try to keep the game at a brisk pace to make it enjoyable.

• In a different colour, write the vowels separately on the flip-chart and explain that a vowel is always the middle phoneme of a word with three phonemes. Can the children think of some more CVC words themselves? If they can, let them write the words on the flip-chart, or scribe for them. Ask each child to name the middle phoneme of their word, or instead focus on one of the children, asking the group, 'What's the middle phoneme of Simon's word?'

• Play a game with the magnetic letters in the feely bags. Let different children take one letter out of each bag and put it onto the magnetic board to make a CVC word. Nonsense words are allowed. Can the children read the words they have made? Have some fun making up silly meanings for the nonsense words. For example, 'dop' could be a lollipop for a dog.

• Look at the words with the same onset, which you wrote on the flip-chart before the session. Together, read the words and then ask the children 'What's the same about all these words?' When they have realised that the beginnings of the words sound the same, encourage them to come to the flip-chart and write the words again, using a different colour for the onsets. Explain that the correct name for the beginning of a word is *onset*. Play a game where the children have to think of words with different onsets from the ones on the flip-chart. For example, if you wrote *cap*, *can*, *cat*, *cash* and *catch*, the children might suggest *tap*, *pan*, *mat*, *bash* and *hatch*. According to achievement level, you could use their suggestions to make lists of words with the same onset, including nonsense words. For example, using *tap* as the starter word, you could have *tan*, *tat*, *tash* and *tatch*; *pan* could give *pap*, *pat*, *pash* and *patch*, and so on.

- Look at the words with the same rime, which you wrote on the flip-chart before the session. Together, read the words and then ask the children 'What's the same about all these words?' Encourage them to come up and write the words again, using a different colour for the rimes. Explain that the correct name for the end of a word is *rime*, but this is a different word from *rhyme*. Play a game where the children have to think of words with different rimes from the ones on the flip-chart. For example, if you wrote *cat, hat, mat, pat, flat, that* and *chat*, the children might say *cap, had, man, pan, fly, this* and *chop*. According to achievement level, you could use their suggestions to make lists of words with the same rime, including nonsense words. For example, using *cat* as the starter word, you could have *bat, dat, fat, grat, tat* and *slat*; *man* could give *ban, dan, pan, ran* and *stan*, and so on.

Focus activities

Group A: Give the magnetic letters plus board and CVC picture cards (face down) to the children. Let them play a game where they turn over a picture card, sound the phonemes and make the word on the board with the magnetic letters.

Group B: Draw five columns on the flip-chart and head them with the vowels; put the CVC cards face down on the table. Play a game where the children pick a card, say the word aloud and then tell you the medial phoneme, before fixing the card in the right column on the flip-chart, using the Blutack.

Group C: Put the CVC cards face down on the table. Let the children play a game where they turn over a card and then think of a CVC word that rhymes, including nonsense words. For example, if they turn over the picture of a man, they could say *ban, can, fan, pan, han, jan, yan* and so on.

Group D: Let the children place magnetic letters *ch, t, p, th* and *w* on one side of the magnetic board and *in* on the other. Ask them to match up both sets of letters to make words. Can they recognise the common rime and the different onsets? Change the rime to *op* and then *at*, and challenge the children to show you the nonsense words.

Group E: Together, make a collection of objects and/or pictures with the same rime, for a table display, e.g. a cat, a mat, a bat and a hat. The children could write labels for each object, using different colours to highlight the onset and rime.

Other structured play activities

- Use vowel cards and a stopwatch or egg timer to play a game. You show a vowel and set the timer, and the children have to think of as many words as they can within the time limit.
- Using old newspapers, ask the children to cut out letters from the headlines to make some CVC words. They should stick their letters onto white or yellow paper.
- Let the children play a game of 'Fishing' with CVC fish cards. They take turns to use their fishing-rods to catch a fish and read the CVC word on it. If they are right, they keep the fish; if not, they throw it back into the pond.
- Make duplicate sets of CVC words to play snap or pelmanism.
- Let the children use felt-tipped pens to write CVC words, onsets and/or rimes onto inflated balloons and hang these from the ceiling.
- Let the children have fun writing freely on the board or flip-chart, making words using a common rime, e.g. *in, en, ip, at* and so on. Do the same with onsets, e.g. *ca, te, pi, en, ch* and so on.

© 2003 Collette Drifte, *Literacy Play for the Early Years* (Book 4), David Fulton Publishers Ltd.

© 2003 Collette Drifte, *Literacy Play for the Early Years* (Book 4), David Fulton Publishers Ltd.

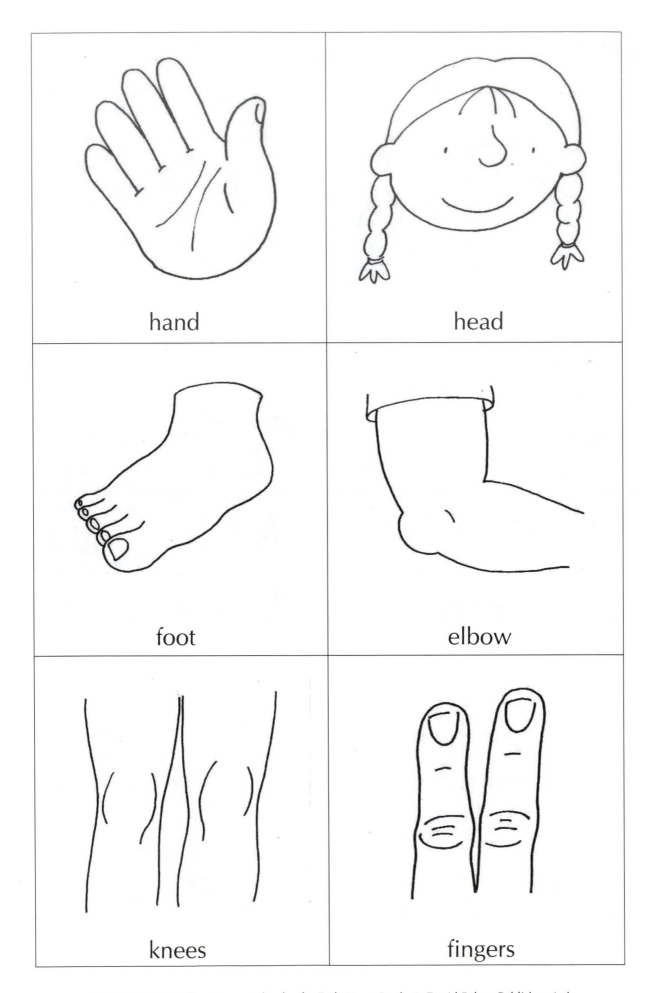

hand

head

foot

elbow

knees

fingers

© 2003 Collette Drifte, *Literacy Play for the Early Years* (Book 4), David Fulton Publishers Ltd.

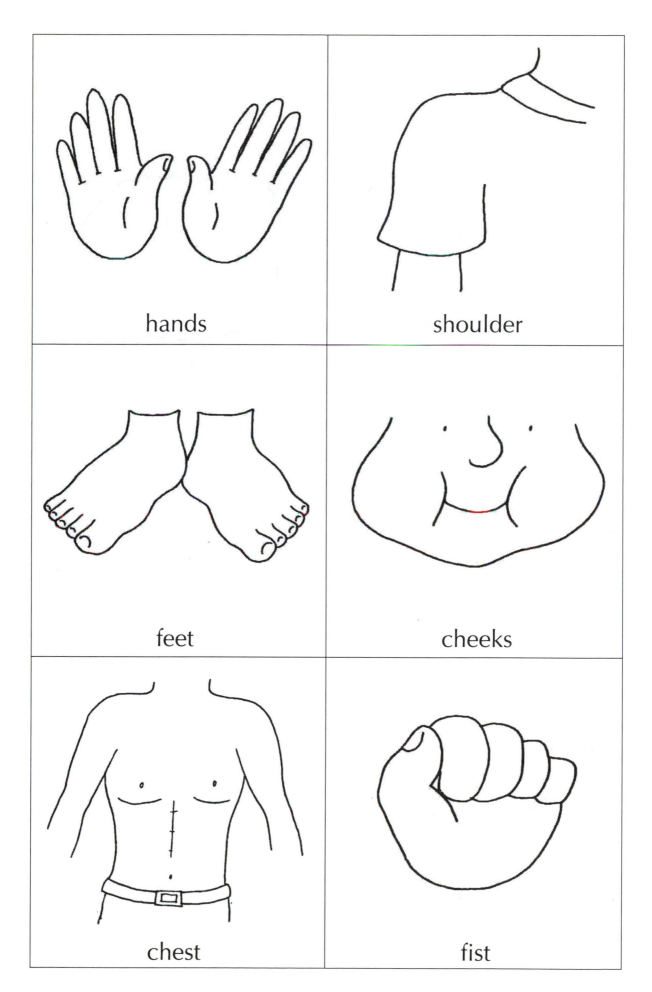

hands

shoulder

feet

cheeks

chest

fist

© 2003 Collette Drifte, *Literacy Play for the Early Years* (Book 4), David Fulton Publishers Ltd.

happy

sad

surprised

angry

© 2003 Collette Drifte, *Literacy Play for the Early Years* (Book 4), David Fulton Publishers Ltd.

sleepy

telling to be quiet with finger on lips

afraid

disappointed

© 2003 Collette Drifte, *Literacy Play for the Early Years* (Book 4), David Fulton Publishers Ltd.

Group-sound card 1: vehicles

© 2003 Collette Drifte, *Literacy Play for the Early Years* (Book 4), David Fulton Publishers Ltd.

Group-sound card 2: animals

© 2003 Collette Drifte, *Literacy Play for the Early Years* (Book 4), David Fulton Publishers Ltd.

Group-sound card 3: weather

© 2003 Collette Drifte, *Literacy Play for the Early Years* (Book 4), David Fulton Publishers Ltd.

Group-sound card 4: the house

© 2003 Collette Drifte, *Literacy Play for the Early Years* (Book 4), David Fulton Publishers Ltd.

© 2003 Collette Drifte, *Literacy Play for the Early Years* (Book 4), David Fulton Publishers Ltd.

© 2003 Collette Drifte, *Literacy Play for the Early Years* (Book 4), David Fulton Publishers Ltd.

© 2003 Collette Drifte, *Literacy Play for the Early Years* (Book 4), David Fulton Publishers Ltd.

CHAPTER 2

Year 1

PHONIC FOCUS

Medial vowels

Objectives from the *National Literacy Strategy*:

- To discriminate and segment all three phonemes in CVC words.
- To secure identification, spelling and reading of initial, final and medial letter sounds in simple words.

Materials needed

- Flip-chart and marker pens, magnetic board and letters, two feely bags, stopwatch or egg timer, a selection of CVC objects such as a hat, a pen, a top, a cup, a van, a peg, a tin, a mop and a jug
- Alphabet cards, CD player and CD accompanying this book, vowel cards for each child in Group B, tokens
- Stimulus objects (see 'Preparation'), large sheet of paper, pencils or marker pens
- Old magazine or newspaper (see 'Preparation'), scissors
- Snakes and ladders board, vowel cards, tiddlywinks, die

Optional materials for other activities

- Five large sheets of paper, each with a vowel written on it, Blutack
- *Progression in phonics: materials for whole-class teaching* (DfEE 1999, 2000)

Preparation

- ▲ Familiarise yourself with the term *medial vowels*, i.e. short-sounding vowels in the middle of CVC words. For example, ham, leg, sip, hot and jug.
- ▲ Put the vowels on the magnetic board; put a selection of consonants into the feely bag; put the CVC objects into the second feely bag; write a list of CVC words on the flip-chart without their vowels, e.g. *c–t, p–n, c–p, p–g* and so on; divide the second page of the flip-chart into five columns, each headed with a vowel.
- ▲ Prepare a set of alphabet cards for Group A – you might like to take out of the consonant pack cards such as *q, x* and *z*. Sort the cards into two piles, consonants and vowels.
- ▲ Collect a set of stimulus objects with CVC names, two for each vowel. For example, a hat and a pan, a peg and a pen, a tin and a lid, a box and a mop, a jug and a cup.
- ▲ Divide a large sheet of paper into five columns, each headed with a vowel.
- ▲ Enlarge a page of an old magazine or newspaper on a photocopier for each child in Group D.

Introducing the phoneme

- Can the children remember what 'phoneme' means? Remind them that it's the proper term for the sound a letter makes. Can they remember the vowels and their phonemes? Play a game with the magnetic letters by asking different children to identify the vowel after you have said the phoneme. Play the game in reverse by asking children to tell you the phoneme of vowels you point to. Have some fun by asking different children to take two consonants out of the feely bag and make a CVC word with one of the vowels. Let them make nonsense words.

- Play a game where you take an object out of the feely bag and the children take turns to name the medial phoneme. Invite them to come up and write the name of the phoneme on the flip-chart – they should then point to the medial vowel and say again what its phoneme is.

- Look at the incomplete CVC words on the flip-chart and ask the children to choose a vowel to complete each word. Can they think of several words from the same unfinished one? For example, c–p could give cap, cop or cup and p–n could give pan, pen, pin or pun. Leave the flip-chart available for the children to add more words during unstructured times – tie a pen to the easel with some string.

- Turn to the second page of the flip-chart and ask the children to read the vowels aloud. Play a game using the stopwatch or egg timer. Different children have to write on the flip-chart a word in the column that you name. For example, Colin, write a word with the medial vowel 'o' or Sandeep, write a word with the medial vowel 'u'. How many words can the children write within the time limit set by you or the egg timer? Can they improve their record in subsequent games?

Focus activities

Group A: Play a game with the alphabet cards where the children take two cards from the consonant pile and one from the vowels. If they can make a word they keep the cards; if not, the cards go back to the bottom of the pile.

Group B: Give a set of vowel cards to the children and play a game. Listen to track 13 of the CD accompanying this book. The first child to hold up the correct vowel card in response to the questions on the CD wins a token. The winner is the child with the highest number of tokens at the end of the game.

Group C: Give the stimulus objects to the children and ask them to make rhyming chains for each. Tell them that nonsense words are allowed. For example, for box and mop, they could have fox, cox, jox, bop, nop, sop and so on. They should write their words in the appropriate columns on the chart. Leave the chart available and encourage them to add to it later as they think of more words – tie a pen to the easel with some string.

Group D: Give the enlarged magazine page to the children and ask them to cut out all the CVC words and sort them into the five vowel groups. Can they make sentence(s) using the words? Can they make sentence(s) using one word from each pile?

Group E: Give the children the snakes and ladders board, die, tiddlywinks and vowel cards, face down on the table. Let them play a game where they shake the die and move their tiddlywink along in the usual way. When they reach the base of either a snake or a ladder, they take a vowel card and say a CVC word with the vowel on the card as the medial phoneme. If they are correct, they can go up the snake or ladder. (They don't come back down a snake, even if they land on its head.) The winner is the child who reaches the top first.

Other structured play activities

- Fix large vowels to the wall in different parts of the hall. Play a game where the children stand in the centre of the hall and you call out a CVC word. The children have to run and stand under the appropriate vowel for that word. For example, if you call out *jug*, the children all stand under the *u* sheet. The last two or three children to reach the position are eliminated and the winners are the children who 'survive' the longest.
- Play 'Grandma Went to Market' where the names of all the items Grandma buys are composed of CVC words. The child also has to sound the vowel phoneme.
- Play *Circle Swap Shop* or *Match Me* as outlined in *Progression in phonics: materials for whole-class teaching* (DfEE 1999, 2000).
- Let the children use highlighter markers to identify the medial vowels in CVC words on an enlarged page from a magazine. They should use a different colour for each vowel. For example, red for all the 'a's, blue for all the 'e's and so on.

PHONIC FOCUS

Final consonant digraphs

Objectives from the *National Literacy Strategy*:

- To investigate, read and spell words ending in *ff, ll, ss, ck* and *ng*.

Materials needed

- CD player and CD accompanying this book
- Flip-chart and marker pens, pictures of/or objects that end with the focus digraph (see 'Preparation')
- Card, scissors, pens or marker pens
- Focus phoneme and beginning cards (see 'Preparation')
- Cassette recorder/player, blank cassette, pictures of objects that end with the focus digraph

Optional materials for other activities

- *Progression in phonics: materials for whole-class teaching* (DfEE 1999, 2000)
- Focus phoneme and beginning cards (see 'Preparation')

Preparation

- ▲ Familiarise yourself with the meaning of the term *final consonant digraph*, i.e. two or more consonants together that make one phoneme and that are at the end of a word. For example, so**ck**, wi**sh**, gla**ss**, mo**th**, ca**tch** and cou**gh**. Listen to track 14 of the CD for correct pronunciations.
- ▲ Have prepared the pictures, or display the objects that end with the focus digraph, for example a bell and a doll, a glass and a dress, a sock and a duck or a ring and a swing.
- ▲ Make two sets of cards, one with the focus final consonant digraph written on each card and the other with different beginnings (for a list of relevant words see Figure 2.1).

Introducing the digraph

This is a general session that can be used for any of the digraphs. You may choose to explore different digraphs over several sessions:

- Look at the objects or pictures of things that end with the focus digraph and talk about their names. Does anyone know what phonemes they end with? Explain to the children that we use the word *digraph* when two letters together make one phoneme. (Children enjoy using technical terms and it is important that they become familiar with and confident in using the terms used in the literacy curricula.) Tell them that today they're going to explore the final consonant digraph *xx*. Can they tell you why it's called a final **consonant** digraph? Can they suggest why it's called a **final** consonant digraph?
- Tell the children you're all going to play the 'Word-clapping game'. The children are allowed to say nonsense words as long as the focus final consonant digraph is correct and

they're also allowed to 'pass' if they're stuck. Sit in a circle and start a slow handclap. Once the rhythm has been established, say three or four words ending with the focus final consonant digraph, then point to one of the children who adds an additional word. Then the next child says a different word, and so on until everyone has had a go, all the time keeping the rhythmic slow handclap going.

- Play a game of 'Digraph Football'. Divide the children into two football teams (let the children choose which ones). One by one ask the children whether a word and/or picture ends with the focus phoneme. For example, *Andrew, does 'sniff' end with 'ff'?* or *Daniel, does 'glass' end with 'ff'?* If their answers are correct, they score a goal. The winning team is the one that scores the highest number of goals.
- Challenge the children to write on the flip-chart as many words as they can think of that end with the focus final consonant digraph. Have fun making up some silly sentences that link two or more of their words. For example, *My nose went stiff after a sniff* or *The boy ate grass from a glass plate.* Leave the flip-chart available so the children can add new words during unstructured sessions. Tie a pen on a string to the easel.

Focus activities

Group A: Help the children to make word slides or word circles (see Figures 1.8 and 1.9) and play with them to make words with the focus final consonant digraph.

Group B: Help the group to make word searches to include words with the focus final consonant digraph (see Figure 2.2). Let the children give each other their word searches to complete.

Group C: Give the children the focus final consonant digraph cards and the different beginnings cards face down on the table. Let them play a form of pelmanism where they turn over two of the cards and if they can make a word, they keep the pair. Nonsense words are allowed, as long as the child can identify and read the final consonant digraph.

Group D: Play a game of 'I hear with my little ear, something ending with . . .', using the focus final consonant digraph as the clue. Ask each child to say a word – nonsense words are allowed and the children are allowed to 'pass' if they wish – and accept any word that has the correct final consonant digraph. You could initially help the children in their choice by displaying cards with the words written on them.

Group E: Give the cassette recorder, blank cassette and pictures to the children. Ask them to record rhyming chains for each picture, starting each chain with *This is a . . . and it rhymes with . . .* For example, *This is a king and it rhymes with ring, sing, bring, wing, swing, sting, spring, thing, string and cling.*

Other structured play activities

- Play *Croaker* as outlined in *Progression in phonics: materials for whole-class teaching* (DfEE 1999, 2000), focusing on the required phonemes.
- Make two sets of cards, one with the focus final consonant digraph written on each card and the other with different beginnings. Let the children play a game where they match the two sets to make nonsense words and then give them silly definitions. For example, *spa* and *ng* make *spang*, which means to bounce up and down on a big rubber spring, or *gra* and *ff* make *graff*, which is an animal that looks like a green giraffe.

- Use vowel cards and a stopwatch or egg timer to play a game. You show a final consonant digraph and set the timer, and the children have to think of as many words as they can within the time limit.
- Make a spinning top (see Figure 3.3 on p. 81) with a phoneme on each face. Play a game where the children take turns to spin the top and read the phoneme, give a word beginning or ending with the phoneme and/or say and/or write a sentence that includes the words. Tailor the game according to the children's achievement level.
- Let the children have fun writing freely on the board or flip-chart, making words using a focus final consonant digraph and different beginnings.

ck	ff	ll	ss	ng
clock	sniff	bell	glass	long
duck	stiff	pull	grass	ring
sock	stuff	shell	mess	song
black	fluff	well	dress	bang
sack	muff	doll	kiss	king
brick	huff	ball	address	sing
stick	bluff	mill	class	hang
rock	cuff	gull	less	bring
block	cliff	bull	pass	wing
lick	whiff	spell	press	swing
lock	off	pull	across	sting
lack		smell	chess	spring
neck		fall	bless	thing
kick		wall	miss	string
back		stall	bliss	strong
sick		hall	hiss	gang
shock		still	boss	rang
flock		tell	cross	cling
crack		frill	moss	wrong
track				along
wick				pong
chick				oblong

Figure 2.1 Words with the final consonant digraphs *ck*, *ff*, *ll*, *ss* and *ng* for Year 1

Find these words in the word search. They all have the final consonant digraph *ck*. You may go across or down. One has already been done for you.

lick	m	o	t	c	s	b	c	m	l
sock	f	e	c	k	o	i	b	i	i
lock	l	o	c	k	c	c	a	c	c
neck	t	l	e	c	k	k	c	k	k
~~kick~~	u	t	o	~~k~~	~~i~~	~~c~~	~~k~~	a	n
back	s	i	c	k	c	k	l	o	e
sick	c	k	f	a	c	k	c	k	c
shock	c	k	m	o	s	h	o	c	k

(Note: You can make a word search more challenging by having the words also read upwards and backwards.)

Figure 2.2 An example of a word search

Initial consonant blends and clusters

Objectives from the *National Literacy Strategy*:

- To discriminate, read and spell words with initial consonant clusters.
- To identify separate clusters within words containing clusters in speech and writing.
- To blend phonemes in words with clusters for reading.
- To segment clusters into phonemes for spellings.

Materials needed

- CD player and CD accompanying this book
- Flip-chart, marker pens, objects or pictures of things that begin with the focus initial blend or cluster (see 'Preparation')
- Initial consonant blend or cluster cards, word ending cards (see 'Preparation'), card, glue, scissors
- Paper, pens or marker pens, cassette recorder and blank cassette (optional), sorting trays
- Draughtsboard and draughtsmen, initial consonant blend or cluster cards
- Bingo cards (see 'Preparation'), covers, list of words with focus blend(s) or cluster(s)
- Blend-tubes (see 'Preparation'), string

Optional materials for other activities

- A4 paper, marker pens
- CD player and CD accompanying this book, initial consonant blend or cluster cards matching the blends or clusters on track 15 of the CD (alternatively, have single letter cards)
- *Progression in phonics: materials for whole-class teaching* (DfEE 1999, 2000)

Preparation

- ▲ Familiarise yourself with the term *initial consonant blends and clusters*. A blend consists of two letters giving two phonemes. For example, **gl** as in *gloves*. Because it is at the beginning of the word, it is an initial consonant blend. A cluster consists of three letters giving three phonemes. For example, **str** as in *straight* is an initial consonant cluster. Listen to track 14 of the CD for the correct pronunciations.
- ▲ Prepare the pictures or display the objects that begin with the focus blend or cluster, for example a **gl**ove, **gl**ue, a **gl**obe and a **gl**ass or a **sk**ate, a **sk**irt, **sk**ittles, **sk**is and a **sk**eleton.
- ▲ Draw two columns on the flip-chart. Write the focus initial consonant blends or clusters down the left-hand side and appropriate word endings down the right-hand side (see Figure 2.3).
- ▲ Make initial consonant blend or cluster cards and word ending cards – for a list of words with the focus initial consonant blends or clusters, see Figure 2.4.
- ▲ Use Photocopiable Sheet 14 (p. 69) to make a set of bingo cards with a focus blend or

cluster in the squares to be matched (see Figure 2.5); cut out enough small covers for the children to blank off called squares on their cards; have a selection of words that tie up with the blends or clusters on the bingo cards (see Figure 2.4).

▲ Cut cardboard tubes into small pieces and write on each one a consonant blend or cluster, or a word ending. For example, *gl* on one piece and *oves* on another, and so on. Make sure you tie up both the blends or clusters and the word endings.

Introducing the blend or cluster

This is a general session that can be used for any of the phonemes. You may wish to take several sessions over this work, tackling blends first and then clusters:

- Talk about the objects or pictures of things that begin with the focus blend or cluster, exploring the name of each one. Can anyone tell you what blends they begin with? Explain to the children that we use the words *blend* when two letters together make two phonemes, and *cluster* when three letters together make three phonemes. (Children enjoy using technical terms and it is important that they become familiar with and confident in using the terms used in the literacy curricula.) For example, *sk* as in **skeleton**, **skis** and **skirt**, *gr* as in **grass**, **green** and **granny**, or *str* as in **straw**, **string** and **street**. Tell them that today they're going to explore the initial consonant blend *xx* or cluster *xxx*. Can they tell you why it's called an initial **consonant** blend or cluster? Can they suggest why it's called an **initial** consonant blend or cluster?

- Look at the two columns on the flip-chart and ask the children to blend the phonemes. Can they join the beginnings and the endings to make the complete words? Let the children write the words on the flip-chart themselves. Can they think of more words beginning with the focus blend(s) or cluster(s)? Let them add these to the list. Have some fun playing charades where different children mime one of the words and the others have to guess which it is. Then together, make some nonsense words by joining the initial consonant blends and other endings – challenge the children to make up silly definitions for the new words.

Focus activities

Group A: Ask the children to make a list of words with the focus blend or cluster, then use some of them to make an alliterative phrase or sentence. Tell them that their sentences can be silly, as long as they feature the blend or cluster being explored. Let them write or record their sentences and phrases for the others to read or listen to.

Group B: Give the objects, trays and initial consonant blend or cluster cards to the children and ask them to sort the objects into the same blend or cluster groups and put them into the trays together with the correct initial blend or cluster card.

Group C: Let the children play a game with the draughtsboard, draughtsmen and blend or cluster cards face down on the table. They take turns to pick a card and if they can say a word beginning with that initial consonant blend or cluster, they move their draughtsman forward one space. The first child to reach the other side of the board is the winner.

Group D: Give the children the bingo cards. Call a word and the children have to cover the square with that initial consonant blend or cluster, if it is on their card. The winner is the first child to have a Full House.

Group E: Give the children the cut-up cardboard tubes and string. Ask them to pair the pieces of tube together to make words with initial consonant blends or clusters. They should then thread them together with the string. Hang the tube-words along the walls as a display.

Other structured play activities

- Write different initial consonant blends and word endings on A4 paper, to make pairs. Fasten a sheet on each child's back and play a game where the children all go around reading the sheets on each other's backs, until they can pair up with someone to make a word. For example, a child with *str* on her back could pair up with one who has *ap* on his, or yet another who has *ing*.
- Let the children listen to track 15 of the CD that accompanies this book. They could use either the initial consonant blend or cluster cards, or the single letter cards to carry out the activity.
- Use chalk to draw a hopscotch-type grid on the playground, with a blend or cluster in the squares. (Put duplicates in the squares where the children will land with both feet.) The children can play a form of hopscotch where they call out the blend or cluster in each square they jump into. You can make the grid as long or short as you wish, adding further blends or clusters as more are learnt. You could make the game more challenging by asking the children to call out both the blend or cluster and a word beginning with it.
- Make a word wall with each line of bricks dedicated to a specific blend or cluster. Let the children write a word in each brick with a blend or cluster for that particular line. They can add to the wall any time they discover new words.
- Play *Phoneme Count* as outlined in *Progression in phonics: materials for whole-class teaching* (DfEE 1999, 2000), focusing on the required blends or clusters.

Divide the flip-chart into two columns, with initial consonant blends and appropriate word endings, for the children to make words. For example:

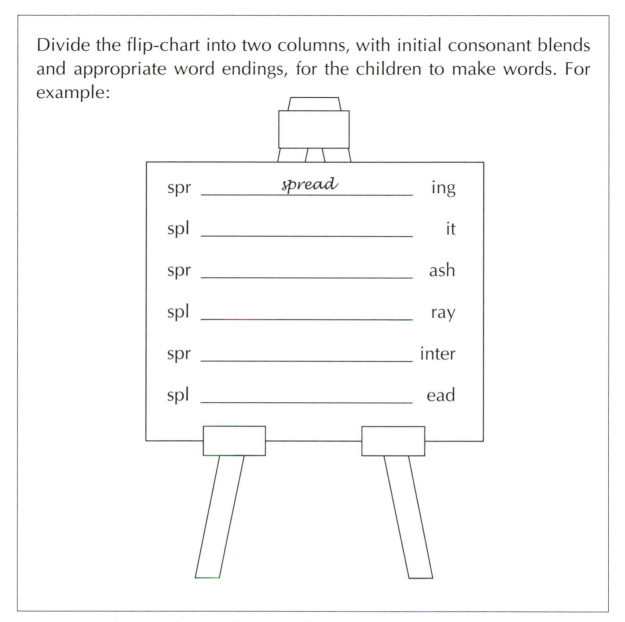

spr _____ *spread* _____ ing

spl _____ it

spr _____ ash

spl _____ ray

spr _____ inter

spl _____ ead

Figure 2.3 Make complete words by matching these beginnings and endings

bl: black, blame, blank, blanket, bleed, blend(er), blind(fold), blink, block, blonde, blood, bloom, blow, blue, blunt, blush

br: bracelet, bracken, brag, brain, brake, branch, brandy, brass, brave, bread, break, breath(e), breeze, brick, bridge, bright, brim, bring, broke(n), brooch, brook, broom, brother, brown, bruise, brush

cl: clap, class, claw, clean, clear, click, cliff, climb, cling, clip, cloak, clock, close, cloth(es), cloud, clover, clown, club, clue, clump, clumsy

cr: crab, crack(er), cramp, crane, crash, crawl, crazy, cream, crease, creature, creep, crib, criminal, crinkle, crisp(s), croak, crocodile, crook, crop, cross, crowd, crown, cruel, crumb, crumpet, crunchy, crust, cry

dr: drab, drag, dragon, drain, draught, draw(er), dread, dream, dress, drill, drink, drive(r), drop, drug, drum, dry

fl: flag, flake, flame, flap, flash, flat, flavour, flea, fleece, flesh, flight, flippers, float, flood, floor, flour, flow, flower, fluff, fluid, flutter, fly

fr: fraction, fragile, frame, free, freeze, fresh, fret, fridge, friend, fright, fringe, frog, from, front, frost, frown, fruit, fry

gl: glacier, glad, glance, gland, glare, glass, glider, glint, globe, glory, glove(s), glow, glue

gr: grab, grain, grammar, gran(ny), grapes, graph, grasp, grass, grate, grave, gravel, gravity, gravy, graze

pl: place, plaice, plain, plan, plane, planet, plant, plaster, plastic, plate, platform, play, pleasant, please, pleasure, plenty, plot, plough, plug, plum, plumber, plump

pr: practice(se), prairie, praise, pram, pray, precious, present, press, pretend, pretty, pretzel, price, prick, prince(ss), print, private, prize, proper(ly), proud

sc: scab, scald, scales, scalp, scampi, scan, scar, scarf, scarlet, score, scout

sk: skate(s), skeleton, ski(s), skid, skill, skin, skip, skirt, skittles, skull, sky

sl: slam, slap, slate, slave, sledge, sleep, sleeve, slice, slide, slip, slope, slow, slug, sly

Figure 2.4 Words with initial consonant blends and clusters for Year 1 phonics

sm: smack, small, smart, smash, smell, smile, smoke, smooth, smudge

sn: snail, snake, snap, snatch, sneak, sneeze, sniff, snip, snore, snow, snuffle, snuggle

sp: space, spade, spaghetti, span, spaniel, spare, spark, speak/spoke, spear, special, speck, spectacles, speech, speed, spell, spend, spice(y), spider, spill, spin, spinach, spine, spiral, spit, spoil, sponge, spooky, spoon, spot, spout, spur, spy

st: stab, stable, stage, stain, stale, stall, stamp, stand, staple, star, stare, start, starve, station, statue, stay, steady, steal, steam, steel, steep, steer, step, stereo, stew, stick, stiff, still, sting, stir, stitch, stocking, stole, stomach, stone, stood, stop, store, storm, story, stuck, student, study, stump, style

sw: swallow, swamp, swan, swap, swarm, swear, sweat, swede, sweep, sweet, swell, swift, swim, swing, switch, swoop

scr: scramble, scrap, scrape, scratch, scrawl, scream, screen, screw, scribe, script, scrounge, scrub, scruff(y)

spl: splash, splendid, splinter, split, splutter

spr: sprat, sprawl, spray, spread, spring, sprinkle, sprint, sprout, spruce

squ: squad, squander, square, squash, squat, squeak, squeeze, squib, squid, squint, squirrel, squirt

str: straight, strain, strand, strange, strap, straw, strawberry, stray, streak, stream, street, strength, stress, stretch, strict, stride, strike, string, strip, stripe, stroke, stroll, strong, struggle

tr: trace, track, tractor, trade, traffic, tragedy, trail, train, tram, tramp, transfer, transparent, transport, trap, travel, tray, tread, treasure, treat, tree, trench, trial, triangle, tribe, trick, trifle, trip, troll, trolley, trombone, trouble, trough, trousers, trout, truck, trudge, true, trunk, trust, try

tw: tweezers, twelve, twenty, twice, twiddle, twig, twinkle, twins, twist, twitch

shr: shred, shrew, shriek, shrill, shrimp, shrink, shrub, shrug

thr: thread, threat, three, thrilling, throat, throb, throne, through, throw, thrush, thrust

Figure 2.4 cont'd

spare	spin	spy		spoil
speak		spider		span
			spear	

Figure 2.5 An example of a bingo card for initial consonant blends

Final consonant blends and clusters

Objectives from the *National Literacy Strategy*:

- To discriminate, read and spell words with final consonant blends.
- To identify separate clusters within words containing clusters in speech and writing.
- To blend phonemes in words with clusters for reading.
- To segment clusters into phonemes for spellings.

Materials needed

- Flip-chart and different coloured marker pens, objects or pictures of things that end with the focus blend or cluster (see 'Preparation'), acetate sheet(s), stopwatch or egg timer
- Final blend or cluster word cards, *Yes* and *No* cards (see 'Preparation')
- Final blend or cluster die (see 'Preparation'), tokens
- Feely bag, magnetic boards and letters
- Fishing-rods with magnets on the end, a pond (see 'Preparation'), blend or cluster fish cards (see 'Preparation'), card, paper-clips
- Sticky notes (see 'Preparation')

Optional materials for other activities

- Sheets of paper with chosen final blends or clusters written on them in large print, Blutack
- *Progression in phonics: materials for whole-class teaching* (DfEE 1999, 2000)
- CD player and CD accompanying this book, final blend or cluster cards, or single letter cards

Preparation

- ▲ Familiarise yourself with the term *final consonant blends and clusters*. A blend consists of two letters giving two phonemes. For example, **sp** as in *wasp*. Because it is at the end of the word, it is a final consonant blend. A cluster consists of three letters giving three phonemes. For example, **rst** as in *first* is a final consonant cluster. Listen to track 14 of the CD accompanying this book.
- ▲ Collect some objects or pictures of things that end with the focus blend or cluster (e.g. a be**lt** and some sa**lt**, a wa**sp** and a cri**sp** or lu**nch** and a be**nch**).
- ▲ Write some words with the same final consonant blend or cluster on the flip-chart. According to the stage reached, you could have a mixture of blends or clusters; write one word with the focus blend or cluster at the top of the next page of the flip-chart.
- ▲ Make two sets of word cards with the focus final consonant blend(s) or cluster(s) (see Figure 2.6 for a list of appropriate words). Make *Yes* and *No* cards for each child in Group A.
- ▲ Use Photocopiable Sheet 15 (p. 70) to make a die with a final blend or cluster written on each face.

▲ Make a pond by bending a rectangle of card into a cylinder and fastening it; make a set of cards in the shape of fish, with a blend or cluster written on each one; fasten a paper-clip onto each fish.

▲ On a series of sticky notes, write some beginnings of words and some final blends or clusters. For example, *pi*, *ca*, *gra*, *sta*, *mp*, *st*, *tch*, *rst* and so on.

Introducing the blend or cluster

This is a general session that can be used for any of the phonemes. You may wish to take several sessions over this work, tackling blends first and then clusters:

• Talk about the objects or pictures of things that end with the focus blend or cluster, exploring the name of each one. Can anyone tell you what blends they end with? Explain to the children that we use the words *blend* when two letters together make two phonemes, and *cluster* when three letters together make three phonemes. (Children enjoy using technical terms and it is important that they become familiar with and confident in using the terms used in the literacy curricula.) For example, *st* as in *last*, *mist* and *just*, *nk* as in *wink*, *tank* and *drink*, or *rst* as in *first*, *worst* and *thirst*. Tell them that today they're going to explore the final consonant blend *xx* or cluster *xxx*. Can they tell you why it's called a final **consonant** blend or cluster? Can they suggest why it's called a **final** consonant blend or cluster?

• Look at the groups of words written on the flip-chart and ask different children to sound the phonemes. Cover the words with an acetate sheet and ask for volunteers to come and draw a circle around the focus final consonant blend(s) or cluster(s). Set the stopwatch or egg timer and challenge the children to add as many new words to each group as they can. Play a second game with a different blend or cluster and try to beat the first game's record.

• Turn to the single word on the next page of the flip-chart. Have some fun with the children changing its beginning to make new words, including nonsense words, leaving the final blend or cluster intact. For example, from *wasp*, you could make *wisp*, *wusp*, *wosp*, *wesp*, *nasp*, *pasp*, *gasp*, *fasp* and so on; from *lunch* you could make *lanch*, *lench*, *linch*, *lonch*, *punch*, *gunch*, *tunch*, *bunch* and so on.

Focus activities

Group A: Play a game with the word cards and the *Yes* and *No* cards. Hold up a word card for the children to decide whether it's a real word. If it is, they hold up their *Yes* card; if not, they hold up their *No* card. Whoever correctly shows a *Yes* or *No* card first, holds up the next word card.

Group B: Play a game with the blend or cluster die, where the children take turns to roll the die and say a word with the final blend or cluster on the uppermost face. If the word is real, the child takes a token and the winner is the person with the most tokens at the end of the game.

Group C: Use the magnetic boards and letters, word cards and feely bag to play a game. Take a word card from the feely bag and read it aloud. The children have to put the correct letters onto the magnetic board to spell the word. The first child to spell it correctly takes the next word card out of the feely bag.

Group D: Let the children play a game of 'Fishing' with the blend or cluster fish cards. They take turns to use their fishing-rods to catch a fish, read the blend or cluster on it and then say a word ending in that blend or cluster. If they are right, they keep the fish; if not, they throw it back into the pond.

Group E: Let the children use the sticky notes to play about with the beginnings and final blends or clusters to make words. Tell them that nonsense words are allowed as long as the children can read and spell them correctly and the final blends or clusters are not altered. They should make a list of the words they devise.

Other structured play activities

- Fix sheets with final blends or clusters to the wall in different parts of the hall. Play a game where the children stand in the centre of the hall and you call out a word with one of the final blends or clusters. The children have to run and stand under the appropriate sheet for that word. For example, if you call out *pink*, the children all stand under the *nk* sheet. The last two or three children to reach the position are eliminated and the winners are the children who 'survive' the longest.
- Play *Quickwrite* from *Progression in phonics: materials for whole-class teaching* (DfEE 1999, 2000).
- Let the children listen to track 16 of the CD that accompanies this book. They could use either the final consonant blend or cluster cards, or the single letter cards to carry out the activity.
- Let the children type words that include the focus blend or cluster on the computer, using the largest possible font, and print them out. Fasten the words to the ceiling and let the children have fun reading the words while lying on the floor. You could also put the words in unexpected places such as at the top of climbing apparatus, on the back of the cloakroom doors or under the sink, to give the children a fun learning experience and word reinforcement.
- Give each child a card with the beginning of a word, or a final consonant blend or cluster. The children should go around reading each other's cards until they find someone they can pair up with to make a word. When they have all found their partner, they should read out their completed word to the others.
- Play the 'Word-clapping game'. The children are allowed to say nonsense words as long as the final blend or cluster is correct and they're also allowed to 'pass' if they're stuck. Sit in a circle and start a slow handclap. Once the rhythm has been established, say three or four words ending with the focus final blend or cluster, then point to one of the children who adds an additional word. The next child then says a different word, and so on until everyone has had a go, all the time keeping the rhythmic slow handclap going.

ct: act, affect, afflict, aquaduct, architect, collect, conflict, connect, convict, correct, derelict, detect, district, direct, effect, eject, elect, evict, expect, fact, infect, inflict, inject, insect, inspect, instruct, neglect, object, obstruct, pact, perfect, predict, product, project, protect, reflect, reject, respect, select, strict, subject, suspect, verdict, viaduct

ft: aircraft, craft, croft, daft, drift, gift, left, lift, loft, raft, shift, sift, snowdrift, soft, swift, theft, tuft

ld: bald, build, child, cold, field, fold, gold, held, hold, mild, mould, old, scald, scold, sold, told, wild, world

lf: elf, engulf, golf, gulf, my/him/her/itself, selfish, shelf, wolf

lk: bulk, elk, hulk, milk, silk, sulk, whelk

lp: gulp, help, yelp

lt: adult, assault, belt, bolt, built, catapult, colt, consult, difficult, felt, fault, guilt, halt, hilt, insult, jolt, kilt, knelt, melt, moult, pelt, result, revolt, salt, smelt, somersault, spilt, stilt, tilt, vault, volt, wilt

mp: camp, damp, dump, jump, lamp, pump

nd: and, band, bandage, bend, bond, hand, land, lend, mend, pond, sand, send, wand

nk: bank, junk, pink, sink, tank, wink

nt: ant, bent, hunt, lent, pant(s), sent, sentence, tent, want, went

pt: adapt, adopt, crept, slept, swept, wept

sk: desk, flask, mask, task, tusk, whisk

sp: crisp, lisp, rasp, wasp

st: best, cast, cost, dust, fast, fist, just, last, list, lost, mast, mist, must, past, pest, post, rest, rust, test, vast, vest, west, zest

xt: next, text

nch: bench, crunch, lunch, munch, pinch

lth: filth, health, wealth

Figure 2.6 Words with final consonant blends and clusters for Year 1 phonics

PHONIC FOCUS

Long vowels

Objectives from the *National Literacy Strategy*:

- To learn the common spelling patterns for each of the long vowel phonemes.
- To identify phonemes in speech and writing.
- To blend phonemes for reading.
- To segment words into phonemes for spelling.

Materials needed

- Flip-chart and marker pens, objects or pictures of things with the focus long vowel in the names (e.g. a wheel and a sheep, a chain and a train, a goat and a toad, and so on), large word circle showing the focus phoneme (see 'Preparation'), card, scissors, fastener, easel
- Snap cards (see 'Preparation')
- CD player and CD accompanying this book (see 'Preparation'), set of picture cards to accompany the CD (see 'Preparation')
- Phoneme die (see 'Preparation'), counters
- Plastic alphabet letters, stopwatch, list of phoneme(s) as required
- Enlarged page(s) of old magazines or newspapers, coloured marker pens, paper and pens, scissors, glue, coloured backing paper

Optional materials for other activities

- Objects or pictures illustrating the focus phoneme(s)
- *Progression in phonics: materials for whole-class teaching* (DfEE 1999, 2000)
- Long vowel picture cards (see Photocopiable Sheets 16–18, on pp. 71–73)

Preparation

- ▲ Familiarise yourself with the meaning of the term *vowel digraph*, i.e. two or more vowels together that make one phoneme. For example, sheep, nail, glue, bough and precious.
- ▲ Make a large word circle (see Figure 1.9 on p. 28) and fasten it to the easel.
- ▲ Make some picture snap cards – have a mixture of things with the focus phoneme in their names and others with different phonemes; make sure there are enough of the focus phoneme to make matching pairs for the game of snap (see Figure 2.7 for a list of long vowel words).
- ▲ Have the CD player with the CD ready to play at track 17; make a set of long vowel picture cards using Photocopiable Sheets 16–18 (pp. 71–73).
- ▲ Make a die using Photocopiable Sheet 15 (p. 70) and write a vowel digraph or long vowel on each face, as required.
- ▲ Enlarge page(s) of an old magazine or newspaper for Group E.

Introducing the phoneme

This is a general session that can be used for any of the phonemes. You will probably spend several sessions working on the different phonemes:

- Look at the objects or pictures of things featuring the focus phoneme and talk about them together. Can anyone tell you what the names of the objects have in common? Ask someone to come and write the phoneme on the flip-chart. Can anyone remember what *digraph* means? (When two letters together make one phoneme.) Can the children tell you what *vowel digraph* means? What are the vowels in the phoneme you are exploring now? What are their short sounds when written individually? How does this change when they become long vowel phonemes?
- Play a game of 'True or False', using the focus phoneme as the basis. For example: *Susan, 'moon' has the vowel digraph 'oo' in it – true or false?; Iqbal, 'jump' has the vowel digraph 'ea' in it – true or false?; Philip, 'cake' has the long vowel 'a–e' in it – true or false?; or Chang Yin, 'hop' has the long vowel 'o–e' in it – true or false?*
- Spend a bit of time exploring the long vowel in more detail. Can the children identify the short vowel sounds of the components of each vowel digraph? For example, *iou* is made up of *i* as in *hit*, *o* as in *hot* and *u* as in *hut*, but as a vowel digraph its phoneme is *u* as in *hut*. Can the children tell you how 'magic e' changes the short vowels? Challenge them to list as many words as they can for each vowel. They may realise that *u–e* can be sounded as in *rude* and also as in *cube*.
- Have some fun with the word circle, asking volunteers to spin it around to see how many words they can make. List the real words down one side of the flip-chart and the nonsense words down the other. Can the children read the nonsense words, remembering to sound the long vowel? Do any of them have a long vowel in their names? For example, Colleen, Stacey, Jane, Charlene and so on.

Focus activities

Group A: Play snap with the children using picture snap cards, but 'snapping' only with the pictures whose names include the focus phoneme, i.e. ignoring the pictures that have a different phoneme or long vowel in their names.

Group B: Place the picture cards that accompany the CD (track 17) face up on the table. Let the children play a game where they listen to the instructions on the CD and the first child to point to the correct card 'keeps' it. The winner is the child with the most cards at the end of the game.

Group C: Give the phoneme die and counters to the children. Let them play a game where they take turns to roll the die. When the die stops, the 'roller' has to read the phoneme on the uppermost face and then say words that have the phoneme in them. The children win a counter for every word they can think of. The child with the most counters at the end of the game is the winner.

Group D: Give the plastic letters and phoneme list to the children. Set the stopwatch to the required time (for example, five minutes) and challenge the children to make words with the set phoneme(s). They should list their words. Can they beat their record on second and subsequent games?

Group E: Get the children (or pairs of children) to share an enlarged page of a magazine and look for words with the focus phoneme. When they find one, they should circle it with a coloured marker pen. According to achievement level, they could look in a dictionary for the words they find. Let them cut out the words and stick them onto coloured backing paper to make a phoneme collage.

Other structured play activities

- Help the children to make a 'word tree' for the focus phoneme. The trunk of the tree should be labelled with the focus vowel digraph or long vowel and the leaves should have a word written on them which contains the focus phoneme. Let the children add more leaves to the tree as they find new words.
- Play 'Treasure Hunt' where you challenge the children to find objects or pictures in the room with the focus phoneme(s) in their names.
- Play *Rhyming Word Generation and Word Sort* from *Progression in phonics: materials for whole-class teaching* (DfEE 1999, 2000).
- Ask the children to make a collection of objects or pictures of things whose names have the focus phoneme in them. Display these while the children are still exploring the phoneme.
- Let the children play the game featured on the CD (track 17) using the picture cards that accompany the CD track.
- Deal the long vowel picture cards (Photocopiable Sheets 16–18) among the children and tell them to find their 'phoneme partner'. They should go around until they find the child who has the card that makes a pair with their own, for example the two *oo* pictures or the two *a–e* pictures.
- Let the children make word wheels using Photocopiable Sheet 19 (p. 74), word slides (see Figure 1.8 on p. 27), word banks, word walls and bingo games (see Figure 2.5) to consolidate the focus phoneme in a fun way.

---

ea: beach, beans, beat, cheat, clean, clear, defeat, eat, flea, heat, lead, leaf, meal, mean, meat, neat, pea(s), peach, please, seat, scream, steam, stream, tea, tear (as in 'cry'), treat

ee: bee, cheese, feel, feet, free, freeze, knee(s), peel, preen, queen, queer, see, sheep, sleep, sleet, squeeze, steep, sweep, teeth, tree, wheel, wheeze

ai: again, brain, chain, complaint, drain, fail, faint, grain, hail, jail, mail, main, nail, paid, pail, pain, paint, plain, rail, rain, snail, stain, tail, trail, train

a-e: bake, blame, cake, came, cane, crane, fade, fake, fame, game, made, make, mane, name, pane, plane, rake, same, shame, take, tame, tape, wake

Figure 2.7 Words with long vowels for Year 1 phonics (grouped according to phoneme)

ay: anyway, bay, clay, day, display, hay, holiday, lay, m/May, mislay, pay, play, ray, say, stay, stray, today, tray, way, x-ray

ie: applied, cried, dried, fried, occupied, qualified, spied, tried

i-e: beside, bite, bride, decide, dine, fine, fire, hide, kite, mine, pine, pipe, pride, ride, seaside, shine, side, slide, stride, tide, time, wide, wine

igh: bright, fight, flight, fright, goodnight, knight, light, midnight, might, night, plight, quite, right, sigh, sight, slight, tight

y: apply, by, cry, dry, fly, fortify, fry, July, lullaby, my, notify, occupy, pry, sky, sly, spy, supply, terrify, try, why

oa: boat, (char)coal, coach, coat, croak, float, foal, goal, goat, groan, Joan, load, loaf, loan, moan, moat, overload, road, roam, soap, stoat, toad, throat, unload

o-e: armhole, bone, buttonhole, close, code, compose, cone, diagnose, dose, expose, foxhole, froze, hole, home, joke, mole, nose, note, phone, poke, pole, postcode, rode, rose, stone, stroke, tadpole, those, throne, vote, whole, wrote

ow: arrow, blow, bow, bowl, crow, elbow, flow, glow, grow, low, mow, owe, pillow, rainbow, row, show, slow, snow, sow, throw, tow

oo: afternoon, baboon, balloon, bamboo, bassoon, boot, cartoon, choose, cocoon, cool, cuckoo, drool, fool, hoof, igloo, maroon, monsoon moon, mushroom, noon, pool, proof, roof, school, shampoo, shoot, soon, spoon, stool, sunroof, too, tool, typhoon, zoo

u-e: accuse, amuse, confuse, cube, cure, cute, dune, enthuse, excuse, fortune, fuse, granule, introduce, mule, mute, produce, pure, reduce, refuse, tube, tune, use

ew: Andrew, brew, chew, crew, dew, drew, few, flew, grew, knew, mildew, new, screw, shrew, stew, threw, unscrew, withdrew, yew

ue: argue, blue, clue, due, pursue, statue, tissue, true, value

Figure 2.7 cont'd

© 2003 Collette Drifte, *Literacy Play for the Early Years* (Book 4), David Fulton Publishers Ltd.

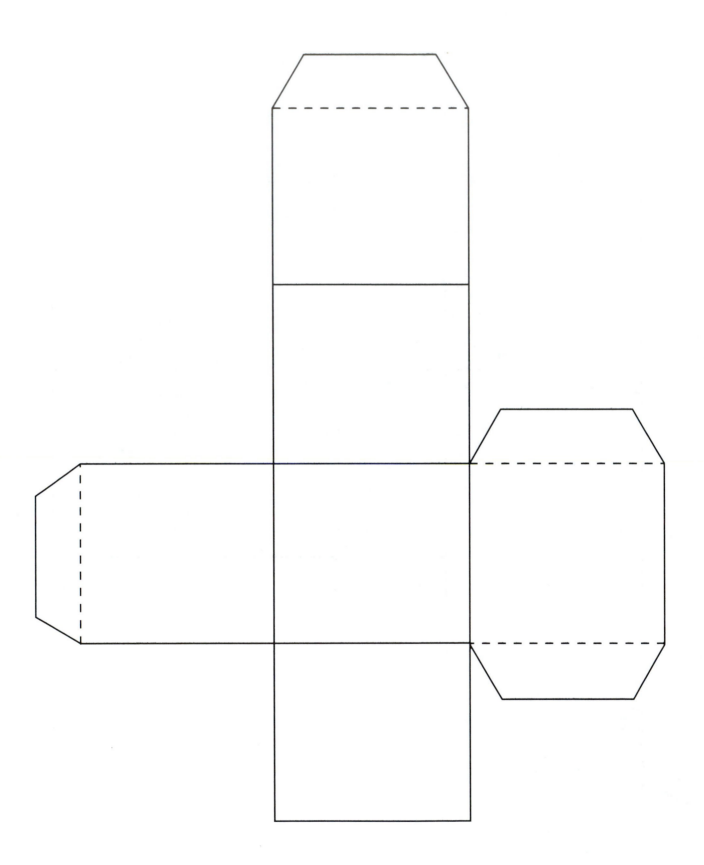

© 2003 Collette Drifte, *Literacy Play for the Early Years* (Book 4), David Fulton Publishers Ltd.

© 2003 Collette Drifte, *Literacy Play for the Early Years* (Book 4), David Fulton Publishers Ltd.

© 2003 Collette Drifte, *Literacy Play for the Early Years* (Book 4), David Fulton Publishers Ltd.

© 2003 Collette Drifte, *Literacy Play for the Early Years* (Book 4), David Fulton Publishers Ltd.

Let the children use this template to make word wheels using the focus phoneme. Write the focus phoneme in the hub and appropriate letters in the rim to enable the children to make words, as in the example below.

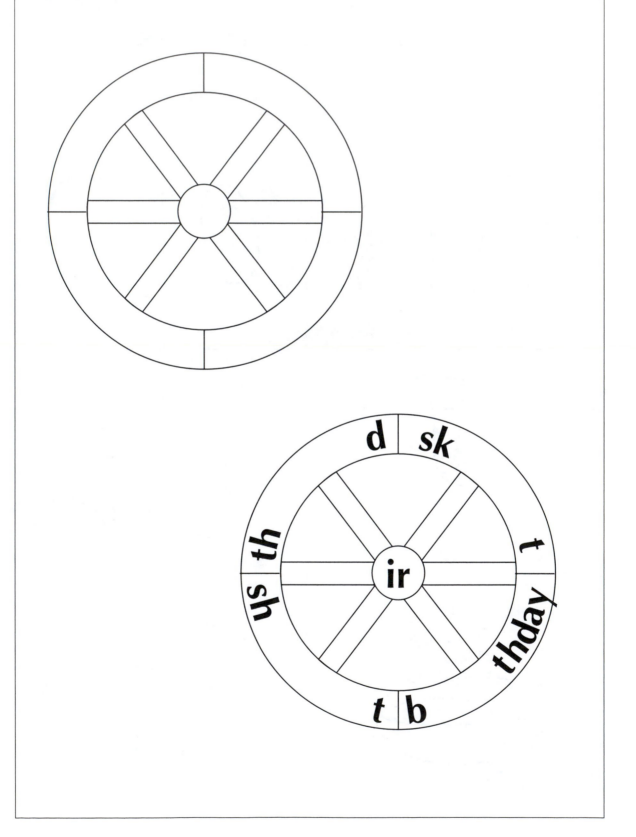

© 2003 Collette Drifte, *Literacy Play for the Early Years* (Book 4), David Fulton Publishers Ltd.

CHAPTER 3

Year 2

PHONIC FOCUS

Vowel phonemes *oo* (short as in *good*), *ar*, *oy/oi* and *ow/ou*

Objectives from the *National Literacy Strategy*:

- To learn the common spelling patterns for the vowel phonemes '*oo*' (short as in '*good*'), '*ar*', '*oy*', '*ow*'.
- To identify the phonemes in speech and writing.
- To blend the phonemes for reading.
- To segment the words into phonemes for spelling.

Materials needed

- ■ CD player and CD accompanying this book
- ■ Figure 3.1 – a list of relevant words
- ■ Flip-chart and coloured marker pens, tokens
- ■ Word wheels (see 'Preparation'), paper, pens or marker pens, scissors, strips of coloured paper, glue, card, spent matches (preferably the very long ones), computer, phoneme segment cards (see 'Preparation') and accompanying word list, cassette recorder/player and blank cassette

Optional materials for other activities

- ■ *Progression in phonics: materials for whole-class teaching* (DfEE 1999, 2000)
- ■ CD player and CD accompanying this book

Preparation

- ▲ Familiarise yourself with the correct pronunciation of the phonemes by listening to track 18 of the CD that accompanies this book.
- ▲ Write the focus phoneme(s) at the top of the first two pages of the flip-chart. Divide the rest of the second page into two columns – in the left-hand column write some words that include the focus phoneme(s); in the right-hand column, write the same words in different positions, leaving out the focus phoneme (see Figure 3.2).
- ▲ Make copies of Photocopiable Sheet 19 (p. 74) for the children in Group A to make their own word wheels.
- ▲ Prepare the strips of paper for making chain links.
- ▲ Make some cards, each showing a segment of a word that features the focus phoneme (e.g. one card with *br*, one with *ow* and one with *n*, to enable the child to make *brown*); write a list of all the words that the cards will make when put together.

Introducing the phoneme

This is a general session that can be used for any of the phonemes. You may choose to explore different phonemes over several sessions:

- Ask the children whether they can remember what the word *phoneme* means. If necessary remind them that we use it when we're talking about the sound a letter makes, i.e. not its name. Do they know what *vowels* are? If memories need to be jogged, spend a few moments talking about vowels. Point to the focus phoneme on the first page of the flip-chart and tell the children that this is the phoneme you're all going to explore today – can anyone tell you what it is? Thoughtstorm some words containing the phoneme and let the children write them on the flip-chart. Encourage them to use a different coloured marker to highlight the focus phoneme. Tell the children you will leave this page open at the end of the session and they may add new words to the list whenever they discover new ones.

- Look at the second page of the flip-chart and use the left-hand column of words to play a game of 'Phoneme Ping Pong': ask Child A to read the first word; Child A reads it and then names Child B to read the next word; Child B reads that and then names Child C, and so on. When putting phonemes into the words in the right-hand column of the page, have some fun by offering alternatives to the focus phoneme and asking the children to tell you whether or not it's a word. For example, if the focus phoneme is *oo* as in *good*, and you're trying to complete *cr - - k*, you might offer *ea* instead of *oo*. Help the children to realise that the word *creak* is a real word, as well as *crook* – the word with the focus phoneme. (When you play this game, make sure you offer only phonemes that the children are already familiar with.)

- Tell the children you're all going to play a game of 'Spell Well'. Cover up the words on the flip-chart, divide the children into pairs or groups of three and have the tokens ready. Choose one of the pairs or groups and say *Who can spell xxx well?* and name one of the words with the focus phoneme. If one of the children in the pair or group spells the word correctly, they win a token. The winners are the group or pair with the most tokens at the end of the game.

- Before finishing the session, turn the flip-chart back to the first page and remind the children that they can add to the list at any time, as long as the words contain the focus phoneme. Leave a pen or pencil on a string tied to the easel.

Focus activities

Group A: Give the children a word wheel and ask them to experiment with the given letters to make words that include the focus phoneme. Let them work in pairs to ask each other how to spell their new words. They should write the words in sentences. According to achievement level, encourage them to look for their new words in a dictionary. Can they tell you the definitions?

Group B: Give the strips of coloured paper to the children and ask them to write a word that includes the focus phoneme on each strip. They should then make a chain with the strips by linking them together and sticking each loop with the glue. Remind them that the word should be on the outside of the link. Hang the chains where the children can read the words – they will have to turn each link to read the word.

Group C: Let the children make spinning tops from card (see Figure 3.3). Let them play a game where they spin the top and then read the phoneme written on the section where it lands. Challenge them to say and/or spell word(s) that include the focus phoneme. If they are correct, they win a token and the winner is the child with the highest number of tokens at the end of the game.

Group D: Ask the group to type words that include the focus phoneme on the computer, using the largest possible font, and print them out. Fasten the words to the ceiling and let the children have fun reading the words while lying on the floor.

Group E: Give the children the cards with phoneme segments and the list of words if the activity is being done independently. Ask the children to put the appropriate cards together to spell the word that either you or one of the children calls out from the list. Challenge them to make up silly sentences that include the words. For example, if they have *br*, *oo* and *k* to make *brook*, they could say, *The man rowed his car in the brook.* Let them record their sentences onto a cassette.

Other structured play activities

- Play *Washing Line* from *Progression in phonics: materials for whole-class teaching* (DfEE 1999, 2000).
- Let the children listen to track 19 of the CD accompanying this book and spell the words. Remind them to switch the player to *Pause* before spelling and/or writing the word(s) and then to switch it on again to check whether they were correct.
- Help the children to make some phoneme kites. The main body of the kite should have the focus phoneme(s) written on it and each tailpiece should have a word that included the focus phoneme(s). Hang the kites from the ceiling. You could even have a go at flying them on a windy day.

---

oo (short): book, cook, hook, look, nook, rook, brook, crook, shook, took, foot, soot, good, hood, stood, wood, wool

ar: alarm, are, artist, bar, barn, car, card, cart, charge, dart, farm(er), garden, hard, harm, harp, jar, mark, market, scar, scarf, shark, sharp, star, start

oi: choice, rejoice, voice, oil, boil, coil, soil, spoil, coin(s), join, joint, point, joist, moist

oy: annoy, boy, convoy, cowboy, destroy, employ, enjoy, joy, loyal, oyster, toy

ou: about, aloud, count, doubt, flour, found, ground, hour, house, loud, mouse, our, out, scour, shout, sound

ow: allow(ed), bow, brown, clown, cow, cowboy, crowd, crown, down, drown, flower, frown, glower, gown, growl, now, owl, shower

air: chair, despair, fair, hair, pair, stair(s)

are: aware, bare, beware, care, compare, dare, declare, fare, glare, hare, mare, nightmare, prepare, rare, scare, share, spare, square, stare

ere: anywhere, elsewhere, everywhere, nowhere, somewhere, there, where

---

Figure 3.1 Words with vowel phonemes and digraphs, and consonant digraphs for Year 2 (grouped according to phoneme)

ear: bear, footwear, knitwear, pear, overbear, sportswear, tear, underwear, wear

or: boring, corn, for, fork, horns, horse, more, north, port, short(s), sort, sport, storm, torch, torn, worn

oor: door, floor, indoor(s), moor, outdoor(s), poor

au: astronaut, caught, daub, daughter, fault, haunt, jaunt, juggernaut, launch, sauna, saunter, taught, taunt, taut

aw: claw, coleslaw, crawl, dawn, draw, drawer, flaw, gnaw, hacksaw, jackdaw, jaw, jigsaw, law, lawyer, outlaw, papaw, paw, prawn, rickshaw, saw, seesaw, shawl, spawn, straw, thaw

ore: before, bore, chore, core, eyesore, forefinger, ignore, implore, more, offshore, restore, score, shore, snore, sore, store, swore, sycamore, tore, wore

er: after, another, brother, danger, driver, farmer, father, hammer, herd, jumper, letter, mermaid, mother, never, other, silver, singer, sister, summer, teacher, tiger, trousers, under, winner, winter

ir: bird, birthday, dirt(y), fir, first, shirt, skirt, squirt, stir, third, thirsty, thirty

ur: burglar, burn, burp, burst, church, curl, fur, hurt, lurch, nurse, slurp, spurt, turn, urn

ch: chaos, character, chasm, chemical, chemist, chemistry, chiropodist/y, chlorine, chlorophyll, choir, cholera, cholesterol, chord, chorus, christening, Christmas, chronic, chronicle, chrysalis, chrysanthemum

ph: phantom, pharmacy, pheasant, phone, phoneme, photocopy, photo(graph), phrase, physics, typhoon

wh: whale, what, wheat, wheel, when, where, which, whiff, while, whine, whip, whisk, whiskers, whisky, whisper, whistle, white, why

ear: appear, clear, dear, disappear, ear, fear, gear, hear, smear, spear, reappear, rear, year

ea: ahead, bread, dead, death, dread, head, lead, overhead, read, shortbread, spread, thread, tread, widespread

Figure 3.1 cont'd

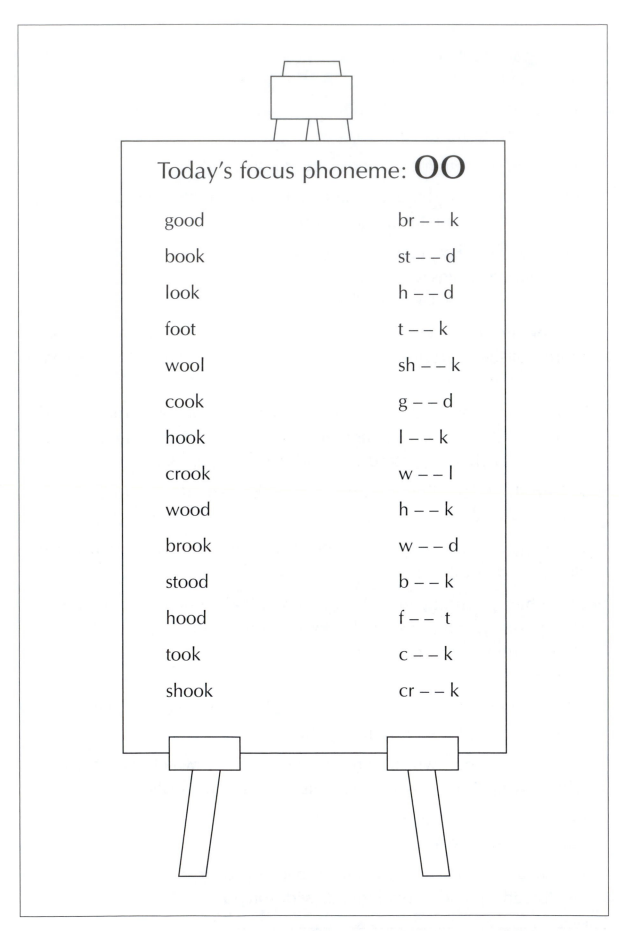

Today's focus phoneme: **OO**

good	br – – k
book	st – – d
look	h – – d
foot	t – – k
wool	sh – – k
cook	g – – d
hook	l – – k
crook	w – – l
wood	h – – k
brook	w – – d
stood	b – – k
hood	f – – t
took	c – – k
shook	cr – – k

Figure 3.2 An example of a flip-chart second page for introducing phonemes in Year 2

Make a spinning top for the focus phonemes, like the one below. Write a required phoneme on each section of the top. Push a spent match through the centre and use the top to play a variety of games.

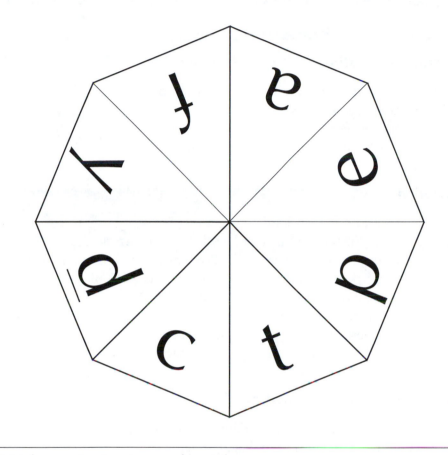

Figure 3.3 Make a spinning top as shown here

PHONIC FOCUS

Vowel phonemes *air/are/ere/ear* (as in *bear*), *or/oor/au/aw/ore* and *er/ir/ur*

Objectives from the *National Literacy Strategy*:

- To learn the common spelling patterns for the vowel phonemes '*air*', '*or*', '*er*'.
- To identify the phonemes in speech and writing.
- To blend the phonemes for reading.
- To segment the words into phonemes for spelling.

Materials needed

- ■ Figure 3.1 – a list of relevant words
- ■ Flip-chart, coloured marker pens, word cards (see 'Preparation'), two feely bags, one glove per child (optional) for 'Jack-in-the-Box', magnetic board and letters including duplicates of those that make up the focus phoneme(s), CD player and CD accompanying this book
- ■ Tortoise templates (see 'Preparation'), pens, scissors, phoneme segment cards (see 'Preparation'), cassette recorder/player and blank cassette
- ■ Word slides (see 'Preparation'), card, scissors, marker pens

Optional materials for other activities

- ■ A selection of phoneme cards, several duplicates with the focus phoneme and some with other familiar phonemes, feely bag, tokens
- ■ String or washing line, pegs, thick paper or thin card, coloured markers, scissors
- ■ CD player and CD accompanying this book

Preparation

- ▲ Write a list of words that include the focus phoneme on the flip-chart. Make a set of cards each with a word written on it, that includes the focus phoneme. Put the cards into one feely bag; put the magnetic letters into the other feely bag. If you play 'Jack-in-the-Box' with a smaller group of children, get them to put on one of their gloves. Have the CD ready to play at track 20.
- ▲ Make tortoise templates from Photocopiable Sheet 20 (p. 94) for each child in Group A.
- ▲ Make some cards, each showing a segment of a word that features the focus phoneme (e.g. one card with *sc*, one with *are* and one with *d*, to enable the child to make *scared*); write a list of all the words that the cards will make when put together.
- ▲ Prepare word slides (see Figure 1.8 on p. 27) for the children in Group D.

Introducing the phoneme

This is a general session that can be used for any of the phonemes. You may choose to explore different phonemes over several sessions:

- Can anyone tell you what the words on the flip-chart say? Ask different children to read them. What do they notice about the words? Point out how the phonemes are the same, even though the letter combination is different in some cases. Can the children identify the focus phoneme(s)? Let them come to the flip-chart and highlight the focus phoneme(s) with a coloured marker pen. Can anyone think of more words for each phoneme? Let them add their words to the list. Tell the children you'll leave the flip-chart and marker pen available and they can add more words to the list whenever they find some. (Leave the pen attached to the flip-chart with a piece of string.)
- Play 'Jack-in-the-Box': take a card out of the feely bag and hold it up for the children to look at; the first 'Jack' to either jump up (smaller groups) or shoot up the hand wearing the glove gets the chance to read the word to you. When the children are correct, they get to take out the next card from the bag and hold it up. (According to achievement level, you could also ask the children to spell the words.) Can the children make up silly sentences for each word?
- Play a game of 'Lucky Dip' where the children take turns to pick a magnetic letter from the feely bag and put it onto the magnetic board. As the letters build up, the children should try to make a word from them, including the focus phoneme. When the children take a letter from the bag that is part of the focus phoneme they can have a 'bonus pick' and take out another letter. Can the children beat their own record in a second and subsequent games? Keep their score on a sheet of paper fastened to the wall.
- Listen to track 20 of the CD and complete the activity verbally, as a whole group.

Focus activities

Group A: Give each child a tortoise template and let the children make their own phoneme tortoises. They should write the focus phoneme in the crown section of the shell and in each of the other sections, they should write a word that includes the focus phoneme. Ask them to check their words in a dictionary and then write a sentence to include the word. They could work in pairs for support.

Group B: Give the children the cards showing the phoneme segments and the list of words if the activity is being done independently. Ask the children to put the appropriate cards together to spell the word that either you or one of the children calls out from the list. Challenge them to make up silly sentences that include the words. For example, if they have *sh*, *or* and *ts* to make *shorts*, they could say, *The horse wore shorts and a tee shirt*. Let them record their sentences onto a cassette and/or write them.

Group C: Ask the children to make a word staircase large enough to go up a wall (see Figure 3.4). Remind the children to write the focus phoneme in a different colour. Tell them they may add new words to the staircase at any time. They could also write sentences in the main body of the staircase in their free time.

Group D: Ask the children to make word slides using words that include the focus phoneme. Let them play with their word slides, to make words that reinforce the focus phoneme.

Group E: Let the children do the listen-and-spell activity on the CD that accompanies this book (track 20). They could do it either verbally or on paper/the whiteboard/the flip-chart, etc.

Other structured play activities

- Put the mixed phoneme cards into the feely bag. Play 'Lucky Dip' where the children take turns to pick a card from the bag and tell you a word that includes the phoneme on the card. If they're correct, they win a token. If they pick out a card with the focus phoneme, when they have told you the word, they can have another 'dip'. The winner is the child with the most tokens at the end of the game.
- Hang a washing-line along one wall of the room. Let the children draw and cut out 'clothes' with the focus phoneme and some words including the phoneme written on them. Challenge the children to make clothes that in themselves illustrate a phoneme. For example, a shirt for *ir*, shorts for *or* or a blouse for *ou*, and so on.
- Let the children listen to the CD that accompanies this book and do the listen-and-spell activity (track 20) in unstructured time without any pressure.

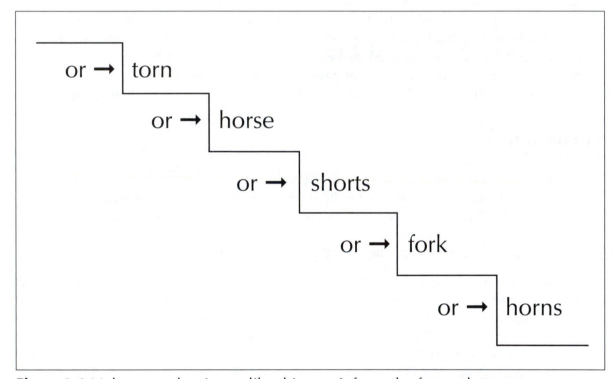

Figure 3.4 Make a word staircase like this to reinforce the focus phoneme

PHONIC FOCUS

Consonant digraphs *wh*, *ph* and *ch* (as in *Christopher*)

Objectives from the *National Literacy Strategy*:

- To read and spell words containing the digraphs '*wh*', '*ph*', '*ch*' (as in *Christopher*).

Materials needed

- ■ Figure 3.1 – a list of relevant words
- ■ Flip-chart and marker pens, dictionary of an appropriate level, segment cards (see 'Preparation'), feely bag, Blutack
- ■ Phoneme boxes (see 'Preparation'), pens, word circles (see 'Preparation'), card, scissors, paper fasteners, segment cards (see 'Preparation'), cassette recorder/player and blank cassette, CD player and CD accompanying this book, word searches featuring words with the focus phoneme(s) (see 'Preparation')

Optional materials for other activities

- ■ Materials to make a word wall, phoneme and segment cards, feely bag, cassette recorder and blank cassette, materials to make bunting, string, CD player and CD accompanying this book

Preparation

- ▲ Write *wh*, *ph* and *ch* on the flip-chart at the top of the page – if possible one page per digraph. On the *wh* page, write the following questions:

  1. ...colour are your eyes?
  2. ...is your Mum's birthday?
  3. ...does a rabbit live?
  4. ...does a baby cry?
  5. ...game do you prefer, tennis or football?

- ▲ On the *ph* page, write *ph* several times in a column; make a set of cards with a segment of a word written on each, for example *ump*, *ant*, *atch*, *ention* and so on.
- ▲ Make a phoneme box sheet for each child in Group A using Photocopiable Sheet 21 (p. 95).
- ▲ Prepare word circles for the children in Group B (see Figure 1.9).
- ▲ Make some cards, each showing a segment of a word that features the focus phoneme (e.g. one card with *ch*, and one with *emist*, to enable the child to make *chemist*.
- ▲ Write a list of all the words that the cards will make when put together; prepare a word search for the children in Group E (see Figure 2.2 on p. 53).

Introducing the phoneme

This is a general session that can be used for any of the phonemes. You may choose to explore different phonemes over several sessions:

- Can the children remember what *digraph* means? If necessary, remind them that when two letters together make only one phoneme, it's called a digraph. Ask the children to tell you some of digraphs they know. Can they tell you what a consonant digraph is? See if they can give you some examples (*ch*, *sh*, *th*, *ff*, *ll*, *rr*, *ss*, *ck* and *ng*). Tell them that today they're going to explore some more consonant digraphs.

- Point to *wh* on the flip-chart and ask the children to tell you what it says. (Be sensitive to regional differences here, since some children may pronounce *wh* as an aspirate, while others may pronounce it as *w*.) Where do they usually see this digraph? Ask them to come and write the words on the flip-chart. If they need a bit of help to start them off, begin a thoughtstorm with words such as *wheel*, *whale* and *whisper* before moving on to *when*, *what*, *which*, *where* and *why*. Spend a bit of time with the children helping them to decide which *wh* words are needed to complete the unfinished sentences. Let them fill in the words themselves. Look at some of the *wh* words in the dictionary and discuss what each one means. If some of the words aren't yet on the list suggested by the children at the beginning of the session, let different children add them.

- Point to *ph* on the flip-chart and ask the children to tell you what it says. Explain that some words and phonemes in English are not regular and this digraph is an example – that *p* and *h* together make the phoneme *f*. Can they tell you some words beginning with this digraph? For example, *phone*, *photo*, *phoneme*, *phantom* or *Philip*. Do they know of anyone called Philip? (The Queen's husband.) Ask them to come and write the words on the flip-chart. Have some fun making up nonsense *ph* words by playing 'Lucky Dip' with the segment cards in the feely bag. (Stick each segment card beside a *ph* on the flip-chart, using the Blutack.) For example, the cards *ump*, *ant*, *atch* and *ention* would give the nonsense words *phump*, *phant*, *phatch* and *phention*. Challenge the children to make up some silly definitions for their words. For example, *phump* could be the noise an elephant makes when it falls over, or *phention* is something that surrounds a garden to keep out stray aeroplanes.

- Point to *ch* on the flip-chart and explain to the children that this digraph looks like one they learnt while they were in Reception Year but its phoneme is completely different. Can anyone suggest how? Explain that this *ch* has the phoneme *k*. Does anyone know a word beginning with this phoneme? For example, *chemist*, *Christmas*, *choir*, *chaos*, *Christopher* or *character*. Let them write their suggestions on the flip-chart and then together explore the dictionary for any more examples. Ask the children for some sentences that include some of the *ch* words you have found.

Focus activities

Group A: Give each child a phoneme box sheet and ask them to fill the box with all the words they can find that have the focus phoneme in them. When they have finished, they should swap 'boxes' and see if their partner found words that they haven't yet discovered. Let them work together to check their words in a dictionary.

Group B: Help the children to make word circles and write onto them words that include the focus phoneme. They should swap their word circles and play with their partner's circle to make words. Let them list the words they make on the appropriate page of the flip-chart.

Group C: Give the children the cards showing the phoneme segments and the list of words if the activity is being done independently. Ask the children to put the appropriate cards together to spell the word that either you or one of the children calls out from the list. Challenge them to make up silly sentences that include the words. For example, if they have *ph* and *otos* to make *photos*, they could say, *The dog showed his holiday photos to the cat.* Let them record their sentences onto a cassette and/or write them.

Group D: Let the children do the activity on track 21 of the CD that accompanies this book. They could work in pairs for support and check each other's spellings.

Group E: Give the children their word search grids and let them do the search either individually or in pairs, according to achievement level. Encourage them to check the words from the grid in the dictionary.

Other structured play activities

- Ask the children to make a word wall, with each row of bricks dedicated to a focus phoneme. The children should write in each brick a word that includes the phoneme for that particular row. Let them add to the wall whenever they find a new word.
- Put all the phoneme and segment cards into the feely bag and let the children have fun playing 'Lucky Dip', making nonsense words from the cards they take out. Let them record their nonsense words onto a blank cassette, reminding them to pronounce the phonemes correctly. They should write a list of their nonsense words so that the other children can listen to the cassette and read the words, during unstructured times.
- Make bunting to string across the room, with each flag displaying a focus phoneme on one side and a word on the other, with the phoneme highlighted in a different colour.
- Let the children do the listen-and-spell activities on track 21 of the CD, in their own time.

PHONIC FOCUS

Vowel phonemes *ear* (as in *hear*) and *ea* (as in *head*)

Objectives from the *National Literacy Strategy*:

*   To discriminate, spell and read the phonemes *ear* (hear) and *ea* (head).

Materials needed

*   ■ Figure 3.1 – a list of relevant words
*   ■ Flip-chart and marker pens, *ear/ea* jingle (see 'Preparation'), stopwatch, dictionary, sticky notes, CD player and CD accompanying this book
*   ■ Word wheels (see 'Preparation'), card, scissors, pens or marker pens, strips of paper, train templates (see 'Preparation'), old newspapers, light-coloured sugar paper, glue

Optional materials for other activities

*   ■ The *ear/ea* jingle, CD player and CD accompanying this book, word cards featuring the focus phonemes

Preparation

*   ▲ Write the *ear/ea* jingle on the flip-chart (see Figure 3.5): you may choose to use only one verse at a time if you are tackling the phonemes in separate sessions. Divide the second page (or third, if you explore the two phonemes at different times) of the flip-chart into three columns; write these word beginnings in the first column: *y, r, p, n, sp, h, t, f, cl, thr, inst, br, spr, d, l, dr*; write *ear* at the top of the second column and *ea* at the top of the third; prepare several sticky notes, each with either *ear* or *ea* written on it; have the CD ready at track 22.
*   ▲ Use Photocopiable Sheet 19 (p. 74) to prepare word wheels for each child in Group A; prepare train templates for the children in Group B using Photocopiable Sheet 22 (p. 96); prepare the strips of paper for making chain links; prepare some old newspapers for cutting up.

Introducing the phoneme

You may choose to explore the two phonemes in different sessions:

*   Look at the jingle on the flip-chart and read it with the children, encouraging them to say it aloud with you. Have some fun reciting the jingle in different ways, such as in rap style, with actions, in the round and so on. Make sure the children are confident about the sounds of both phonemes.
*   Set the stopwatch to a required time (no more than 30 seconds) and challenge the children to think of three *ear* and /or *ea* words in their heads. At the end of the time limit, share the words, letting the children write them on the flip-chart. Can the children also think of some

sentences to include each word? Are there any words that are new to some of the children? If so, spend a bit of time helping the children to look for them in the dictionary, in order to find their meanings.

- When you have explored both phonemes, look at the page on the flip-chart that has been divided into three columns. Have some fun by encouraging the children to experiment with the *ear* or *ea* sticky notes and the word beginnings written on the flip-chart. Let the children take turns to come to the flip-chart and put a sticky note at the end of one of the word beginnings before they decide whether it makes a word. If they're not sure, let them check in the dictionary. When they make a 'real' word, let them write it in the appropriate column. How many words can they come up with? Do any of the word beginnings make words with both phonemes? (They should be able to tell you at least four pairs of words – *hear/head*, *dear/dead*, *drear/dread* and *rear/read*.)
- Play track 22 of the CD that accompanies this book and let the children have some practice at spelling the words with the focus phoneme(s).

Focus activities

Group A: Let the children make word wheel(s), with the focus phoneme(s) written in the hub and appropriate words written around the rim. Challenge them to find words other than those explored during the introductory session.

Group B: Give the children the templates of the train and ask them to write the focus phoneme on the engine and an appropriate word on each carriage. They should make as many carriages as they can.

Group C: Give the children the CD player and the CD that accompanies this book. Ask them to work together to do the listen-and-spell activity on track 22. Challenge them to make sentences for each of the words they spell.

Group D: Give the strips of coloured paper to the children and ask them to take one strip at a time and write a word that includes the focus phoneme(s). They should then make a chain with the strips by linking them together and sticking each loop with the glue. Remind them that the word should be on the outside of the link. Hang the chains where the children can read the words – they will have to turn around each link to read the word.

Group E: Ask the children to cut letters from the headlines of old newspapers to make words with the focus phoneme(s). They should stick the words onto the sugar paper to make collages. Display their work to reinforce the phonemes.

Other structured play activities

- Help the children to learn the two verses of the jingle. Explain that as well as being a fun rhyme, it will help them to remember how to sound the focus phonemes when they're reading.
- Make some word cards using words with the focus phonemes and let the children play Snap or Pelmanism with them.
- Let the children play the CD and complete the listen-and-spell activity on track 22 at leisure.

Don't ever f**ear**
that it's not cl**ear**
how to say the phoneme **ear**;
Just listen here
and you can h**ear**
the same sound with your little **ear**!

Don't shake your h**ea**d.
You don't have to dr**ea**d
the phoneme **ea** you hear in **bread**.
Don't start to fret
or get upset:
it sounds the same as **e** in **bed**!

Figure 3.5 The *ear/ea* jingle

Compound words

Objectives from the *National Literacy Strategy*:

- To split familiar oral and written compound words into their component parts.

Materials needed

- Figure 3.6 – a list of compound words
- Flip-chart and marker pens
- Compound word cards, component word cards and noun cards (see 'Preparation'), card, scissors, feely bag, CD player and CD accompanying this book, cassette recorder/player and blank cassette (optional)

Optional materials for other activities

- Component cards
- CD player and CD accompanying this book
- Materials to make a word bank

Preparation

- ▲ Write several compound words on the flip-chart such as *football, toothbrush, handbag* and *toenail* (see Figure 3.6 for more suggestions).
- ▲ Make a set of cards with a compound word written on each; make two sets of cards with component words that pair up to give a compound word, for example *hand* and *bag, tooth* and *paste* and so on – keep one set in separate piles; make a set of cards with a noun written on each – the nouns should not be related in any way; prepare the CD at tracks 23 and 24.

Introducing the phoneme

- Tell the children that today they're going to have some fun playing with words. Look at the compound words you wrote on the flip-chart and ask the children to read them. Can they spot other words within the compound words? Write on the board the components of each word – *foot* and *ball, tooth* and *brush, hand* and *bag, toe* and *nail*. Tell the children that when a word can be split into other **real** words, the original word is called a *compound word*. Write *compound word* on the flip-chart and read it with the children.
- Play a game where you write a component word and then ask the children to suggest a full (compound) word. For example, you write *head* on the flip-chart and the children could suggest *ache, light, dress* or *first*. Can the children think of more examples of compound words? Let them write these on the flip-chart themselves. Can they write the component words of each of their compound words? Leave the list up and tell the children they may add other compound words they find later on.
- Play a game of 'Compound Word Ping Pong'. You say a component word such as *light* or *man* and the children have to suggest as many compound words as possible. Add an

element of challenge by setting a time limit and seeing whether the children can beat their own record in subsequent games. Keep their score for them to check against later.

- Have some fun making up nonsense compound words. Ask the children to suggest a noun and write it on the flip-chart. Then let them experiment with combinations of two of their suggested words and the meanings. For example, *chair* and *banana*, giving *bananachair* (a chair shaped like a banana) or *chairbanana* (a banana shaped like a chair). Let them have a bit of fun drawing a picture of their favourite compound words.

- Encourage the children to experiment with reversing the order of a compound word, so, for, example, *football* becomes *ballfoot* or *jellyfish* becomes *fishjelly*. Can they give you definitions of the reversed words? Tell them that their definitions can be silly!

Focus activities

Group A: Give the children the compound word cards face down on the table. Let them play a game where they take turns to pick a card and then read the compound word aloud. They then have to tell the others what two words can be found in the compound word. If the others agree, the child keeps the card. The winner is the person with the most cards at the end of the game.

Group B: Let the children listen to tracks 23 and 24 on the CD accompanying this book and complete the activities. They have to split compound words into their components and also make compound words from component words.

Group C: Put the component word cards face up on the table. Ask the children to read the component words and then match the cards to form compound words. They should write these in a list and then make up a sentence for each one. Alternatively, they could record their words and sentences onto a cassette.

Group D: Put the component word cards face down on the table, in their separate piles. Let the children play a game where they take turns to turn over the top card of both piles and see whether they make a compound word. If they don't, one of the cards should be returned to the bottom of its pile and the next child takes the new card off the top of the same pile. If these cards don't make a compound word, the card to be put back is the one which was turned first. In this way, eventually two cards will match to make a compound word. The children should play until all the cards are matched.

Group E: Give the noun cards and feely bag to the children. Let them play a game where they pick one card from the feely bag and make a compound word by adding it to another word of their choice. For example, if they pick a card with *man*, they could write *postman*, *milkman*, *manpower*, *manhole* and so on. They could play in pairs for support and/or use a simple dictionary to help.

Other structured play activities

- Give each child one component card and ask the group to go around reading each other's cards until they find their other half. When everyone is matched up, ask all the children to read out the compound word they make together.

- When you're confident that the children know what compound words are, let them have fun playing around with the components of different words, by swapping them. For example, *toothbrush* and *handbag* make *toothbag* and *handbrush*, or *earring* and *teaspoon* make *tearing* and *earspoon*. Challenge the children to make up definitions for their new words.

- Let the children listen to the relevant tracks on the CD that accompanies this book and do the activities at leisure.
- Ask the children to make a word bank of all the component words and compound words that they discover. Encourage them to use the banks in other areas of work such as poetry.

---

armchair, bagpipe, bathroom, bluebottle, crossroads, daydream, daylight, dishwasher, doormat, downstairs, drumstick, earache, earring, earthworm, eyeball, eyelid, farmhouse, fingernail, fingerprint, fireman, fireside, firewood, fishbowl, flagpole, football, footprint, goalkeeper, goldfish, grasshopper, greenhouse, hairbrush, haircut, handbag, handwriting, headache, headphone, heartbeat, hedgehog, hillside, homesick, homework, housework, indoors, jellyfish, keyhole, kingfisher, kneecap, lifeboat, lifeguard, lighthouse, mealtime, milkman, molehill, moonlight, motorboat, newspaper, nightclothes, notebook, nothing, nowhere, outdoors, overgrown, overnight, pancake, pillowcase, playground, pullover, railway, raincoat, rainfall, rattlesnake, ribcage, riverside, saltwater, sandpaper, sandstorm, sawdust, scarecrow, seafood, seasick, seaside, seaweed, shellfish, shoelace, shoemaker, shopkeeper, signpost, skyscraper, snowball, snowstorm, someone, sometimes, somewhere, spacecraft, spotlight, springtime, starfish, starlight, suitcase, sunflower, sunglasses, sunshine, swordfish, tablecloth, teaspoon, thunderstorm, toothpaste, underground, underwater, upstairs, wallpaper, watchdog, waterfall, waterproof, weekday, weekend, wheelbarrow, wheelchair, windmill, woodwork, workman

---

Figure 3.6 Compound words

Use this template for the children to make word tortoises using the focus phoneme. They should write the focus phoneme at the top of the tortoise's shell and appropriate letters in the other sections, to make words (as in the example below).

© 2003 Collette Drifte, *Literacy Play for the Early Years* (Book 4), David Fulton Publishers Ltd.

Use this template for the children to make phoneme boxes using the focus phoneme. They should write the focus phoneme at the top of the box and then make words (as in the example below).

1.
2.
3.

pl
1.   *please*
2.   *plug*
3.   *plaster*

© 2003 Collette Drifte, *Literacy Play for the Early Years* (Book 4), David Fulton Publishers Ltd.

Use this template for the children to make word trains using the focus phoneme. They should write the focus phoneme on the engine and words on each carriage (as shown in the example below). They can make as many carriages as required.

© 2003 Collette Drifte, *Literacy Play for the Early Years* (Book 4), David Fulton Publishers Ltd.

Observation and assessment for speaking and listening

During your sessions observing the children, you may find it useful to refer to some of these questions as a way of focusing on how their speaking and listening skills are developing:

- Can the children recognise environmental sounds?
- Can the children discriminate between environmental sounds?
- Can the children distinguish between environmental and voice sounds?
- Can they discriminate between different voice sounds?
- Can the children make different voice sounds?
- Can they discriminate between different speech sounds?
- Can the children make different speech sounds?
- Are the grammatical structures correct? Is the syntax correct?
- Do the children use appropriate vocabulary? Do they use context to work out unfamiliar words?
- Do the children show a curiosity about new words and try to explore how to use them appropriately?
- Is their speech fluent and clear?
- Do the children sustain attention when listening?
- Do they listen with respect to others' views and opinions?
- Do the children take turns in conversations?
- Do they make a contribution to the whole-group or small-group discussion?
- Do they appear to understand what is being said by you and by the other children?
- Do the children ask relevant and appropriate questions about a shared text?
- Do the children have a concept of the sequence of a story?
- Do they use the illustrations for clues about the meaning, sequence and content of the story?
- Do the children talk about key events and characters in a familiar story?
- Are they able to negotiate plans and roles?
- Do they enjoy listening to stories, rhymes and songs, and are they able to respond to them, taking part and using them in their play and learning?
- Do the children use language in their imaginative play? Do they role-play and create imaginary experiences?

Observation and assessment for reading and writing

During your sessions observing the children, you may find it useful to refer to some of these questions as a way of focusing on how their reading and writing skills are developing:

- Can the children hear and say initial and final sounds in words? Can they hear and say short vowel sounds within words?
- Can the children name and sound the letters of the alphabet?
- Do the children know that print in English is read from left to right, and from top to bottom?
- Do the children enjoy exploring and experimenting with sounds, words and texts?
- Do they have a knowledge of the vocabulary of literacy, such as 'book', 'cover', 'page', 'line', 'title', 'author', 'front', 'back', 'word', 'reading', 'writing', etc.?
- Can the children write their own name?
- Do they attempt to write for different purposes, such as letters, lists, instructions, stories, etc.?
- Do the children use their knowledge of phonics to attempt to read or write simple regular words?
- Can they hold and use a pencil appropriately?
- Do they write letters using the correct sequence of movements?
- Can the children recognise the important elements of words such as shape, length and common spelling patterns?
- Do the children use different cues when reading, e.g. their knowledge of a story, context, illustrations, syntax, etc.?
- Can they identify significant parts of a text, e.g. captions, characters' names, chants, etc.?
- Are the children aware of the structure of a story, i.e. a beginning, a middle and an end? Are they aware of the actions and consequences within a story?
- Do the children check text for sense? Do they self-correct when something they read does not make sense?
- Can the children identify patterns in stories and poems? Can they extend them?
- Can the children match phonemes to graphemes? Can they write them?
- Do they understand alphabetical order?
- Can the children sight-read familiar words such as captions or high frequency words?

Tracks and/or transcript for accompanying CD

Tracks 1–12 for Reception Year

Track 1

Listen to the sounds. What can you hear?

(doorbell, (ambulance/fire/police) siren, telephone, the wind, car horn, baby crying, thunder, cup and saucer rattling, radio, rain, church bells, motor bike)

Track 2

Listen to the musical instruments. Are they played loudly or softly?

(drum played softly, shaker played loudly, scraper played loudly, woodblock played softly, triangle played softly, drum played loudly, shaker played softly, scraper played softly, woodblock played loudly, triangle played loudly)

Track 3

Listen to the musical instruments. Are they played quickly or slowly?

(drum played slowly, shaker played quickly, scraper played quickly, woodblock played slowly, triangle played slowly, drum played quickly, shaker played slowly, scraper played slowly, woodblock played quickly, triangle played quickly)

Track 4

Can you clap your hands? Press the pause button and do it.

Can you snap your fingers? Press the pause button and do it.

Can you tap your head? Press the pause button and do it.

Can you pat your knees? Press the pause button and do it.

Can you stamp your feet? Press the pause button and do it.

Can you knock on your chest? Press the pause button and do it.

Can you drum with your nails? Press the pause button and do it.

Can you pat your thighs? Press the pause button and do it.

Can you blow through your lips? Press the pause button and do it.

Can you knock your feet together? Press the pause button and do it.

Track 5

We're going to make some voice sounds now. Listen carefully and then press the pause button. Get ready.

Make your voice whiz down a hill. Press the pause button and do it now.

Make your voice sound really shocked. Press the pause button and do it now.

Make your voice jump up and down like a spring. Press the pause button and do it now.

Make your voice feel very sorry for someone. Press the pause button and do it now.

Make your voice sound like a very strong wind. Press the pause button and do it now.

Make your voice sound very frightened. Press the pause button and do it now.

*Make your voice tell everyone to be **really** quiet. Press the pause button and do it now.*

Make your voice sound really happy. Press the pause button and do it now.

Make your voice sound very surprised indeed. Press the pause button and do it now.

Make your voice fly through the clouds. Press the pause button and do it now.

Track 6

Make a voice sound as if you have a pain in your tummy. Press the pause button and make your voice sound now.

Make a voice sound as if you're really angry because someone broke your favourite toy. Press the pause button and make your voice sound now.

Make a voice sound as if you're very, very tired. Press the pause button and make your voice sound now.

Make a voice sound as if something suddenly gives you a big fright. Press the pause button and make your voice sound now.

Make a voice sound as if you're going to be in trouble with your mummy in a minute. Press the pause button and make your voice sound now.

Make a voice sound as if you're very hot. Press the pause button and make your voice sound now.

Make a voice sound as if you're pretending to be a monkey. Press the pause button and make your voice sound now.

Make a voice sound as if you're whizzing down a slide very fast. Press the pause button and make your voice sound now.

Make a voice sound as if you're feeling very cold. Press the pause button and make your voice sound now.

Make a voice sound as if you're really disappointed about something. Press the pause button and make your voice sound now.

Track 7

Let's say 'Baa, baa black sheep' together and clap the rhythm. (Rhyme follows.)

Let's say 'Hickory, hickory dock' together and clap the rhythm. (Rhyme follows.)

Let's say 'Twinkle, twinkle, little star' together and clap the rhythm. (Rhyme follows.)

Let's say 'Mary, Mary, quite contrary' together and clap the rhythm. (Rhyme follows.)

Let's say 'Jack and Jill' together and clap the rhythm. (Rhyme follows.)

Track 8

You're going to make some rhyming chains. Nonsense words are allowed. Let's start off now.

Make a rhyming chain for 'cat' – 'cat'. Now press the pause button.

Make a rhyming chain for 'leg' – 'leg'. Now press the pause button.

Make a rhyming chain for 'tin' – 'tin'. Now press the pause button.

Make a rhyming chain for 'pot' – 'pot'. Now press the pause button.

Make a rhyming chain for 'cup' – 'cup'. Now press the pause button.

Track 9

Let's say 'One wonderful worm' together. Are you ready? After three: 1 – 2 – 3 :

One wonderful worm

Two tootling trumpets

Three thumping thunders

Four fat farmers

Five funny fools

Six sizzling sausages

Seven scrumptious stews

Eight elegant elephants

Nine neon numbers

Ten terrifying tigers

Are coming your way!

Track 10

Correct pronunciation of all YR phonemes: (a-z, ch, sh, th)

Track 11

What's the first phoneme of 'cat' – 'cat'?

What's the first phoneme of 'leg' – 'leg'?

What's the first phoneme of 'pin' – 'pin'?

What's the first phoneme of 'mop' – 'mop'?

What's the first phoneme of 'jug' – 'jug'?

What's the first phoneme of 'bad' – 'bad'?

What's the first phoneme of 'ten' – 'ten'?

What's the first phoneme of 'dig' – 'dig'?

What's the first phoneme of 'lot' – 'lot'?

What's the first phoneme of 'cup' – 'cup'?

Track 12

What's the last phoneme of 'cat' – 'cat'?

What's the last phoneme of 'leg' – 'leg'?

What's the last phoneme of 'pip' – 'pip'?

What's the last phoneme of 'hob' – 'hob'?

What's the last phoneme of 'sun' – 'sun'?

What's the last phoneme of 'wag' – 'wag'?

What's the last phoneme of 'let' – 'let'?

What's the last phoneme of 'bit' – 'bit'?

What's the last phoneme of 'top' – 'top'?

What's the last phoneme of 'mug' – 'mug'?

Tracks 13–17 for Year 1

Track 13

What's the middle phoneme of 'pan' – 'pan'?

What's the middle phoneme of 'beg' – 'beg'?

What's the middle phoneme of 'pit' – 'pit'?

What's the middle phoneme of 'hot' – 'hot'?

What's the middle phoneme of 'bun' – 'bun'?

What's the middle phoneme of 'bag' – 'bag'?

What's the middle phoneme of 'pet' – 'pet'?

What's the middle phoneme of 'bin' – 'bin'?

What's the middle phoneme of 'hop' – 'hop'?

What's the middle phoneme of 'jug' – 'jug'?

Track 14

Correct pronunciation of all Y1 phonemes.

Final consonant digraphs: -'ck', -'ff', -'ll', -'ss', -'ng'

Initial consonant blends and clusters: 'bl' - , 'br' - , 'cl' - , 'cr' - , 'dr' - , 'dw' - , 'fl' - , 'fr' - , 'gl' - , 'gr' - , 'pl' - , 'pr' - , 'sc' - , 'sk' - , 'sl' - , 'sm' - , 'sn' - , 'sp' - , 'spl' - , 'spr' - , 'scr' - , 'squ' - , 'st' - , 'str' - , 'sw' - , 'tr' - , 'tw' - , 'thr' - , 'shr' -

Final consonant blends and clusters: 'ct' - , 'ld' - , 'nd' - , 'lk' - , 'nk' - , 'sk' - , 'lp' - , 'mp' - , 'sp' - , 'ft' - , 'lf' - , 'lt' - , 'nt' - , 'pt' - , 'st' - , 'xt' - , 'nch' - , 'lth' -

Long vowel phonemes: 'ee' - , 'ea' - , 'ai' - , 'a-e' - , 'ay' - , 'ie' - , 'i-e' - , 'igh' - , 'y' - , 'oa' - , 'o-e' - , 'ow' - , 'oo' - , 'u-e' - , 'ew' - , 'ue' -

Track 15

Put out letters to make a word that begins with 'bl' – 'bl'. Press the pause button now.

Put out letters to make a word that begins with 'br – 'br'. Press the pause button now.

Put out letters to make a word that begins with 'cl' – 'cl'. Press the pause button now.

Put out letters to make a word that begins with 'cr' – 'cr'. Press the pause button now.

Put out letters to make a word that begins with 'dr' – 'dr'. Press the pause button now.

Put out letters to make a word that begins with 'dw' – 'dw'. Press the pause button now.

Put out letters to make a word that begins with 'fl' – 'fl'. Press the pause button now.

Put out letters to make a word that begins with 'fr' – 'fr'. Press the pause button now.

Put out letters to make a word that begins with 'gl' – 'gl'. Press the pause button now.

Put out letters to make a word that begins with 'gr' – 'gr'. Press the pause button now.

Put out letters to make a word that begins with 'pl' – 'pl'. Press the pause button now.

Put out letters to make a word that begins with 'bl' – 'bl'. Press the pause button now.

Put out letters to make a word that begins with 'pr' – 'pr'. Press the pause button now.

Put out letters to make a word that begins with 'sc' – 'sc'. Press the pause button now.

Put out letters to make a word that begins with 'sk' – 'sk'. Press the pause button now.

Put out letters to make a word that begins with 'sl' – 'sl'. Press the pause button now.

Put out letters to make a word that begins with 'sm' – 'sm'. Press the pause button now.

Put out letters to make a word that begins with 'sn' – 'sn'. Press the pause button now.

Put out letters to make a word that begins with 'sp' – 'sp'. Press the pause button now.

Put out letters to make a word that begins with 'spl' – 'spl'. Press the pause button now.

Put out letters to make a word that begins with 'spr' – 'spr'. Press the pause button now.

Put out letters to make a word that begins with 'scr' – 'scr'. Press the pause button now.

Put out letters to make a word that begins with 'squ' – 'squ'. Press the pause button now.

Put out letters to make a word that begins with 'st' – 'st'. Press the pause button now.

Put out letters to make a word that begins with 'str' – 'str'. Press the pause button now.

Put out letters to make a word that begins with 'sw' – 'sw'. Press the pause button now.

Put out letters to make a word that begins with 'tr' – 'tr'. Press the pause button now.

Put out letters to make a word that begins with 'tw' – 'tw'. Press the pause button now.

Put out letters to make a word that begins with 'thr' – 'thr'. Press the pause button now.

Put out letters to make a word that begins with 'shr' – 'shr'. Press the pause button now.

Track 16

Put out letters to make a word that ends with 'ld' – 'ld'. Press the pause button now.

Put out letters to make a word that ends with 'nd' – 'nd'. Press the pause button now.

Put out letters to make a word that ends with 'lk' – 'lk'. Press the pause button now.

Put out letters to make a word that ends with 'nk' – 'nk'. Press the pause button now.

Put out letters to make a word that ends with 'sk' – 'sk'. Press the pause button now.

Put out letters to make a word that ends with 'lp' – 'lp'. Press the pause button now.

Put out letters to make a word that ends with 'mp' – 'mp'. Press the pause button now.

Put out letters to make a word that ends with 'sp' – 'sp'. Press the pause button now.

Put out letters to make a word that ends with 'ct' – 'ct'. Press the pause button now.

Put out letters to make a word that ends with 'ft' – 'ft'. Press the pause button now.

Put out letters to make a word that ends with 'lt' – 'lt'. Press the pause button now.

Put out letters to make a word that ends with 'nt' – 'nt'. Press the pause button now.

Put out letters to make a word that ends with 'pt' – 'pt'. Press the pause button now.

Put out letters to make a word that ends with 'st' – 'st'. Press the pause button now.

Put out letters to make a word that ends with 'xt' – 'xt'. Press the pause button now.

Put out letters to make a word that ends with 'lf' – 'lf'. Press the pause button now.

Put out letters to make a word that ends with 'nch' – 'nch'. Press the pause button now.

Put out letters to make a word that ends with 'lth' – 'lth'. Press the pause button now.

Track 17
Pick out the cards that have 'ee' in their name. Press the pause button now.

Pick out the cards that have 'ai' in their name. Press the pause button now.

Pick out the cards that have 'ie' in their name. Press the pause button now.

Pick out the cards that have 'oa' in their name. Press the pause button now.

Pick out the cards that have 'oo' in their name. Press the pause button now.

Pick out the cards that have 'you' in their name. Press the pause button now.

[NB – THESE TO BE PRONOUNCED PHONETICALLY, NOT SPELT.]

Tracks 18–24 for Year 2

Track 18
Correct pronunciation of all Y2 phonemes:

Vowel phonemes: 'oo' - , 'u' - , 'ar' - , 'oi'/'oy' - , 'ow'/'ou' - , 'air'/'are'/'ere'/'ear' - , 'or'/'oor'/'aw'/'au'/'ore' - , 'er'/'ir'/'ur' - , 'ear' - , 'ea' -

Track 19
Spell these words. I'll say each word twice and then you should press the pause button before you write the word. Get ready for the first word.

Book – book. Press the pause button and write the word.

Crook – crook. Press the pause button and write the word.

Foot – foot. Press the pause button and write the word.

Good – good. Press the pause button and write the word.

Wool – wool. Press the pause button and write the word.

Car – car. Press the pause button and write the word.

Farm – farm. Press the pause button and write the word.

Garden – garden. Press the pause button and write the word.

Hard – hard. Press the pause button and write the word.

Start – start. Press the pause button and write the word.

Boy – boy. Press the pause button and write the word.

Joy – joy. Press the pause button and write the word.

Enjoy – enjoy. Press the pause button and write the word.

Boil – boil. Press the pause button and write the word.

Voice – voice. Press the pause button and write the word.

Out – out. Press the pause button and write the word.

Loud – loud. Press the pause button and write the word.

Count – count. Press the pause button and write the word.

Cow – cow. Press the pause button and write the word.

Growl – growl. Press the pause button and write the word.

Track 20

Spell these words. I'll say each word twice and then you should press the pause button before you write the word. Get ready for the first word.

Chair – chair. Press the pause button and write the word.

Scare – scare. Press the pause button and write the word.

There – there. Press the pause button and write the word.

Wear – wear. Press the pause button and write the word.

Fork – fork. Press the pause button and write the word.

Floor – floor. Press the pause button and write the word.

Caught – caught. Press the pause button and write the word.

Straw – straw. Press the pause button and write the word.

Snore – snore. Press the pause button and write the word.

Mermaid – mermaid. Press the pause button and write the word.

Birthday – birthday. Press the pause button and write the word.

Nurse – nurse. Press the pause button and write the word.

Track 21

Spell these words. I'll say each word twice and then you should press the pause button before you write the word. Get ready for the first word.

Christmas – Christmas. Press the pause button and write the word.

School – school. Press the pause button and write the word.

Chemist – chemist. Press the pause button and write the word.

Chorus – chorus. Press the pause button and write the word.

Phone – phone. Press the pause button and write the word.

Photo – photo. Press the pause button and write the word.

Phantom – phantom. Press the pause button and write the word.

Phoneme – phoneme. Press the pause button and write the word.

Wheel – wheel. Press the pause button and write the word.

Whisk – whisk. Press the pause button and write the word.

Whistle – whistle. Press the pause button and write the word.

Whale – whale. Press the pause button and write the word.

Track 22
Spell these words. I'll say each word twice and then you should press the pause button before you write the word. Get ready for the first word.

Fear – fear. Press the pause button and write the word.

Clear – clear. Press the pause button and write the word.

Near – near. Press the pause button and write the word.

Year – year. Press the pause button and write the word.

Disappear – disappear. Press the pause button and write the word.

Head – head. Press the pause button and write the word.

Bread – bread. Press the pause button and write the word.

Dead – dead. Press the pause button and write the word.

Spread – spread. Press the pause button and write the word.

Thread – thread. Press the pause button and write the word.

Track 23
Write the two smaller words you can hear in these compound words. I'll say each compound word twice and then you should press the pause button before you write the two smaller words. Get ready for the first compound word.

Football – football. Press the pause button and write the words.

Daydream – daydream. Press the pause button and write the words.

Grasshopper – grasshopper. Press the pause button and write the words.

Flagpole – flagpole. Press the pause button and write the words.

Seaweed – seaweed. Press the pause button and write the words.

Kingfisher – kingfisher. Press the pause button and write the words.

Sunflower – sunflower. Press the pause button and write the words.

Hedgehog – hedgehog. Press the pause button and write the words.

Pancake – pancake. Press the pause button and write the words.

Handbag – handbag. Press the pause button and write the words.

Track 24
Listen to the two small words I'm going to say and then write the compound word you can make from them. I'll say each set of two smaller words twice and then you should press the pause button before you write the compound words. Get ready for the first set of two smaller words.

Foot and ball – foot and ball. Press the pause button and write the compound word.

Hair and brush – hair and brush. Press the pause button and write the compound word.

Rain and coat – rain and coat. Press the pause button and write the compound word.

Blue and bottle – blue and bottle. Press the pause button and write the compound word.

Sand and paper – sand and paper. Press the pause button and write the compound word.

Gold and fish – gold and fish. Press the pause button and write the compound word.

Sun and glasses – sun and glasses. Press the pause button and write the compound word.

Finger and print – finger and print. Press the pause button and write the compound word.

Pillow and case – pillow and case. Press the pause button and write the compound word.

Life and boat – life and boat. Press the pause button and write the compound word.

JEROME LIBRARY
CURRICULUM RESOURCE CENTER
BOWLING GREEN STATE UNIVERSITY
BOWLING GREEN, OHIO 43403

DATE DUE

		APR 1 5 REC'D	
OCT 2 2 2004			
JA1 11-15			
NOV 2 3 REC'D			
OCT 1 6 2008			
NOV 5 AGG			
NOV 0 5 REC'D			
OhioLINK			
SEP 2 5 REC'D			
OhioLINK			
APR 1 5 2010			
GAYLORD		PRINTED IN U.S.A.	

CURR 372.21 D779Lph

Drifte, Collette.

Literacy play for the early
  years. Learning through
phonics